The Official Christian **Babysitting** Guide

The Official Christian
Babysitting Guide

REBECCA PARK TOTILO

LEGACY PRESS
A Division of Rainbow Publishers

To my dear, sweet daughter, Rachel. You are my inspiration and reason for writing this book. Without your help as "Mom's helper" and baby brothers' babysitter, it wouldn't have been possible.

Special thanks to:
Jude, who clicked the mouse.
Dallas, who kept a tight lid on my notebook computer.
And Dylan, who always let me know what others were doing.

THE OFFICIAL CHRISTIAN BABYSITTING GUIDE
©2001 by Rebecca Park Totilo
ISBN 1-58411-027-9
Legacy reorder# LP48021

Legacy Press
P.O. Box 261129
San Diego, CA 92196

Illustrator: Aline Heiser

Printed in the United States of America

Contents

....

HERE'S THE WAY!

Whether you've been babysitting a long time for your little sister or you just landed your first job babysitting for the next-door neighbor's 4-year-old son, it's important to have the knowledge and skills to be able to handle the many challenges of babysitting.

This book will provide you with all the information for starting and running your own babysitting business. Having a babysitting business is a great way to earn extra cash! But, making money is not what it's all about. For Christians, babysitting goes beyond getting paid to show up and watch TV until the parents get home. It's offering a trustworthy service to your customers while sharing God's love with the kids for whom you are caring.

YOU ARE NEEDED!

Being a Christian babysitter is important. In fact, it's one of the most important jobs ever! When you serve and care for children, you are actually serving God. The Bible says whatever you do for those in need is actually like doing something for Him (check out Matthew 25:40). When you think of it that way, bandaging a scraped arm or hugging a crying child suddenly seems much more significant!

Do you remember what Jesus said when a disciple asked Him who was the greatest in the kingdom of heaven? Jesus called a child over and said, "I tell you the truth, unless you change and become like little children, you will never enter the kingdom of heaven. Therefore, whoever humbles himself like this child is the greatest in the kingdom of heaven. And whoever welcomes a little child like this in my name welcomes me. But if anyone causes one of these little ones who believe in me to sin, it would be better for him to have a large millstone hung around his neck and to be drowned in the depths of the sea" (Matthew 18:3-6). Wow! That's heavy-duty stuff. God really cares about what happens to children and wants you to help them know Him. It's up to you, His servant, to help lead them in the right direction and keep them far from sin.

You will reap great rewards from your babysitting experience, not only in heaven, but here on earth! You will learn valuable lessons on the job, while gaining great work experience. Not to mention earning some extra cash!

WHAT'S iNSiDE...

This manual is filled with helpful hints, cool tips and suggestions to help you become the very best sitter around — the kind parents dream of. It will show you how to find clients, how to handle emergency situations, how to take care of babies and toddlers and how to keep older kids from saying those dreaded words: "I'm bored." Every babysitting job is an adventure when you use the Bible-based crafts, songs, snacks and games in *The Official Christian Babysitting Guide* while you are on the job. Kids will have so much fun, they won't want you to leave!

The *Christian Babysitter's Quiz* on page 11 will help you find out if babysitting is the right job for you. But first, did you pray and ask God if this is something you should do? If not, turn to page 13 for suggestions on creating a quiet time with God that will not only improve your babysitting but make a difference in all areas of your life.

Everything you need to run a successful babysitting business and stay organized is included in this manual: forms, checklists, reminders, safety tips, Scriptures and prayers. But, this manual cannot replace certified training in babysitting or first-aid. The safety tips and first-aid techniques in this book should serve only as reminders for what to do in the case of an emergency. Call your local American Red Cross chapter to find out about courses offered in babysitting, basic first-aid and CPR. Hands-on training will give you the confidence and skills you need to become a really great babysitter.

BABYSITTING:
IS IT RIGHT FOR YOU?

SO YOU THINK YOU'RE READY FOR A JOB? Caring for children is a very important job from God. When parents leave their home, they place you in charge and give you full responsibility for the safety of their children.

Are you saying to yourself, *Yeah, but what does God have to do with that?* Everything! Even though the parents decide to hire you, God is ultimately in control of everything. Nothing gets by Him without His stamp of approval! If you believe that God has an important plan for your life, then you know that you need to pray about babysitting like you would pray about other areas of your life. God gives everyone different skills. Even if you feel He is calling you to babysit, you may need to work on a few skills first.

How prepared are you to be a babysitter? Take this quiz and find out!

THE CHRISTIAN BABYSITTER'S QUIZ

Check yes or no for each question.

1. Did you pray and ask God if you should start a babysitting service?

⦿ Yes ◯ No

If yes, go to #2. If no, then turn to page 13 and read "What Does God Want Me to Do?" before continuing this quiz.

2. Did you get your parents' permission to start babysitting?

⦿ Yes ◯ No

3. Can you take on babysitting without neglecting your homework, after-school activities or church commitments?

⦿ Yes ◯ No

4. Do you enjoy being with young kids?

◯ Yes ◯ No

5. Can you stay calm in tough situations?

　◯ Yes　◯ No

6. Are you patient and kind to others?

　◯ Yes　◯ No

7. Can you handle the responsibility of taking care of someone's children and home?

　◯ Yes　◯ No

8. Do you have the time and energy necessary for babysitting?

　◯ Yes　◯ No

9. Does the idea of changing a messy diaper make your nose wrinkle?

　◯ Yes　◯ No

10. Can you stay friendly and upbeat through hours of temper trantrums and sibling rivalries?

　◯ Yes　◯ No

?????????????????????????????

If you answered **"YES"** to these questions, you are ready for an exciting ministry in babysitting!

If you answered **"no"** to any of these questions, you may need to spend more time with young children in a group setting before you go solo. Try volunteering a few hours each week in your church's nursery. Explain to the nursery director that you want to learn to be a better babysitter. You will be amazed at the hints and tips experienced parents share with you! If you have younger brothers or sisters, ask your parents for "practice time" with them. Start off easy, such as watching your siblings while your parents go away for short periods of time, then build up to babysitting for longer stretches. This gradual increase of time will give you the confidence and practice you need to be able to handle jobs away from home.

WHAT DOES GOD WANT ME TO DO?

Sometimes in our busy lives it can be hard to hear God's voice and know what He wants us to do. Schedule a few minutes now to be alone with God. Find a quiet place to sit with your Bible and be still before God. The Lord is always eager to be with you and He wants to spend time with you. God has a special plan for your life. He is excited about your friendship with Him!

As you plan your quiet times with God, don't allow yourself to be deceived by thoughts like, "God doesn't want to spend time with me because I haven't read my Bible lately." God is always ready to be with you. He wants to help you understand the best way to live. The more time you spend alone with God, the more confident you will be that you are living according to His plan.

Make a commitment now to have a quiet time each day. Fill in the space below with the time you plan to spend alone with God each day.

I WILL HAVE MY QUIET TIME AT _____ EACH DAY.

A WORD on THE WAY

In him we were also chosen, having been predestined according to the plan of him who works out everything in conformity with the purpose of his will.
~ Ephesians 1:11

HOW TO KNOW GOD'S WILL

You might be feeling very sure that it is God's will for you to babysit, or you may be uncertain. There are several ways to find out if you are living within God's will:

1. Pray and spend time with God (see some ideas below).

2. Read your Bible. A Scripture may pop out at you and be the answer you were looking for.

3. Is there an "open" door for you to babysit? Do you have any job offers? Or is the door closed? If God "closes" the door, He has something better for you!

4. Seek godly counsel. Ask your parents, pastor or teacher if they think it is a wise decision for you to start a babysitting business.

5. Do you have a peaceful feeling about babysitting? If not, maybe God wants you to consider other options.

6. Does babysitting fit into the big picture of your life? (See *The Big Picture* on page 17.) For example, if your goal is to be a great gymnast, your time might be better spent practicing in the gym. On the other hand, if you are interested in being a teacher, babysitting is the ideal practice!

AS YOU BEGIN YOUR QUIET TIME

There are no set rules on how to be with God. Sometimes just sitting silently and focusing on Him is enough. Other times you might need some help getting started. Here are some steps for quieting yourself before the Lord:

1. Ask the Lord to reveal anything that may be standing in the way of your hearing His voice. Do you have any sins or grudges you are holding onto? Ask for forgiveness now.

2. Close your eyes and try to concentrate on Jesus. Praise Him!

3. Thank God for being with you.

4. Commit this time to the Lord. Sit quietly and wait for Him to speak.

5. Read a few Scriptures in your Bible, then stop and think about how they apply to your life.

6. Use the *Quiet Time Diary* forms starting on page 219 to take notes during this time.

You will seek me and find me when you seek me with all your heart.
~ Jeremiah 29:13

ASK YOUR PARENTS

It's a good idea to talk and pray with your parents about your desire to start a babysitting business. They can help you determine if you have the time and are ready to work. Your parents will also need to be in on the decision-making process if they will be providing transportation to and from your jobs.

Once you get permission to babysit from your parents, discuss each job offer with them before you accept it. Some jobs may not be right for you, especially if you are just getting started. Your parents can help you decide which jobs are best for you.

After you accept a job, remind your parents for whom you will be babysitting, the time the job starts and the time you will return home. Leave the address and phone number where you can be reached. Let your parents know if you will get a ride from your client or if you will need them to drive you to and from the job.

Make plans by seeking advice.
~ Proverbs 20:18

DO I HAVE TIME?

Time is one of the most important things to consider when starting a babysitting business. Here are some questions to think about:

◎ Will babysitting interfere with activities that are important to you?

◎ Are you allowed to go out on school nights?

◎ How late are you allowed to stay out?

Even if you have limited amounts of time, you

can still be a successful babysitter if you are organized. Fill in the *Babysitter's Calendar* on page 229 with all of your activities throughout the week (make a copy of the blank calendar or scan it into your computer). Include time for studying, church activities and fun with family and friends. Use a colored marker to highlight open times where babysitting might fit in. Don't forget to leave yourself some free time!

THE BiG PiCTURE

How does a babysitting business fit into the big picture of your life? In the TV below, write your goals or draw what you think your future may hold for you.

teacher
day care person
doctor
girl scout leader
nun

LET'S GET DOWN TO BUSINESS!

WORD OF MOUTH is the best way to let people know you are ready to babysit. Tell everyone you come in contact with: relatives, church congregation, neighbors, teachers, your parents' friends and co-workers and your friends who already babysit and can recommend you.

ADVERTISE

To really get noticed, design extra-large business cards using 3" x 5" index cards. Hang them on bulletin boards at places like your church, grocery stores, the local community college, health clubs and the public library.

WHAT TO SAY

Someone spotted your business card on the bulletin board at the grocery store and calls to book you for Friday night. Now what do you do?

First, get the basic information. Use the *Before I Leave Home* form on page 235 to write down your client's name and address with directions on how to get to their home and whether or not they will be providing transportation to and from the job.

If you are not familiar with the family, it would be a good idea to "interview" the parent on the phone and fill in the *Getting to Know You* form on pages 237-243 or you may want to set a time to meet with them in person prior to the job. However, if you already know the family, it is

appropriate to simply go to the job a half-hour early and have the parents show you what needs to be done to care for their kids.

WHAT TO CHARGE

Your babysitting rates should be fair, affordable and consistent with what others are charging. Ask friends who babysit what they charge. The usual rate for babysitting one child is between $2 and $5 per hour.

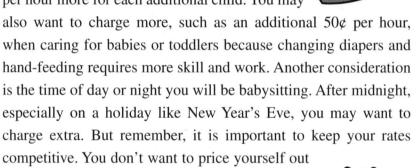

To determine your rate, you should consider how many children you will be caring for. When you care for two or more children, you may charge your normal rate plus a dollar per hour more for each additional child. You may also want to charge more, such as an additional 50¢ per hour, when caring for babies or toddlers because changing diapers and hand-feeding requires more skill and work. Another consideration is the time of day or night you will be babysitting. After midnight, especially on a holiday like New Year's Eve, you may want to charge extra. But remember, it is important to keep your rates competitive. You don't want to price yourself out of business!

If a customer tells you that your rates are too high, ask what they had planned to pay. If the customer says he or she cannot afford your extra charge for late-night services, for example, you may want to waive the extra charge. It's up to you!

TERRIFIC TIP!

CLEAN CASH

Never charge extra for cleaning up a mess you or the kids made. But you can charge $1 for extra cleaning, like vacuuming, if the parents ask you to do it.

~BROOKE, 12, DAYTON, OH

HOW TO GET THERE

If the job isn't within walking distance, or it is dark outside, most clients will pick you up and drive you to their home. Be sure to mention that you will need a ride and arrange a time. If they cannot pick you up, ask your parents before you accept the job if they will be able to drive you. Never walk to or from the job after dark unless an adult goes with you. And never ride with a parent who appears intoxicated or whom you do not trust to drive you for any reason. Instead, respectfully ask if you can use the phone to call your parents to come and get you. Don't worry about losing a client this way — your safety is more important than any babysitting job.

GETTING PAID

Let your customers know you want to be paid at the end of the job. Some parents will forget and come home without the right change to pay you. To avoid this, bring a few extra dollars and coins so you can make change for them.

If the parent doesn't have enough money to pay you, ask him or her what time you can come by the next day to pick up the rest of your earnings. You may want to call that day and remind them you will be coming.

If getting paid at the end of the evening is a continual problem with a customer, or the parents constantly owe you money, you should not accept any work from them until the problem is resolved. Try to maintain mutual respect between you and the customer. For example, you might say to your customer, "With all due respect, I would really appreciate if you could pay me at the end of each job."

If you decide not to accept any more work from a customer, say something like, "I'm not going to be able to help you because my personal policy is that payment is due when the service is given." Do not feel guilty or embarrassed about trying to get paid. The Bible says in Luke 10:7 "for the worker deserves his wages." You've earned it. It's yours! Don't worry, though — most parents are extremely appreciative. They know the value of your service and will be ready to pay you on the spot.

From time to time, you may want to offer your services for free if you are interested in working as a ministry for a family in need. Settle with the parents in advance the number of hours you are willing to offer as a free service.

GIVING BACK

A portion of all the money you earn belongs to God. This is your "tithe," which means one-tenth. The Bible says in Malachi 3:10, " 'Bring the whole tithe into the storehouse, that there may be food in my house. Test me in this,' says the Lord Almighty, 'and see if I will not throw open the floodgates of heaven and pour out so much blessing that you will not have room enough for it.' " When you honor God with your tithe, He will bless you.

Feeling confused about how to figure one-tenth of your income? Let's say you earned $15 from your babysitting job last night. To get one-tenth, take the first two numbers (15) and move the decimal over once to the left, giving you 1.5 or $1.50. Ask a parent or teacher to explain the figures to you if you need help.

Donating free babysitting to a family in need can also be considered part of your tithe. Instead of accepting cash payment, you are giving your time to accomplish God's work. The Lord honors that type of tithe, too.

"Offerings" are gifts over and beyond your tithe. You can make an offering to help others in need or give to missionaries far away. This is something God wants you to do out  of a cheerful heart, not grudgingly. The Bible says in 2 Corinthians 9:7-8, "Each man should give what he has decided in his heart to give, not reluctantly or under compulsion, for God loves a cheerful giver. And God is able to make all grace abound to you, so that in all things at all times, having all that you need, you will abound in every good work." God promises when you do give, He will make sure you always have enough to meet your own needs. God honors obedience!

"For I know the plans I have for you," declares the Lord, "plans to prosper you and not to harm you, plans to give you hope and a future."

~ Jeremiah 29:11

DRESSING THE PART

Now that you are a professional in business for yourself, it's important to dress the part. A simple rule to remember is: wear comfortable clothing that looks neat and clean. Keep in mind that you will be around little kids, which means you could be crawling on the ground, running, cooking or bathing. It would be smart to save that new party dress for a different occasion!

Check out Prepared Paige and Terrible Tess on the next pages to learn about the do's and don'ts of being a beautiful babysitter.

PREPARED PAIGE

◎ A neat, professional appearance lets parents know that you treat your job seriously.

◎ Comfortable shoes will allow you to play with and chase after kids.

◎ Keep long hair neatly tied back and out of the way.

◎ Don't forget to bring your *Official Christian Babysitting Guide* and notebook in case you need a quick refresher course.

◎ Carry your Babysitter's Backpack (see page 28).

◎ Wear a wristwatch to help keep track of feedings, bedtimes and other kid-related schedules.

◎ Tote along a first-aid kit just in case of an emergency.

TERRIBLE TESS

◎ Dangling earrings and necklaces can be grabbed or ripped out by babies.

◎ Chewing gum and blowing bubbles is unprofessional when talking to parents.

◎ The party outfit might look great but it's not babysitter-friendly.

◎ High-heeled shoes are uncomfortable and could cause injury.

◎ Long fingernails can spread germs or scratch the baby. Keep your nails cut short and wash your hands often.

◎ Always come prepared for activities and accidents.

PAIGE

TESS

THE BABYSITTER'S BACKPACK

One way to make your job easier is to have everything you need in one place, ready to go at a moment's notice. Find a backpack you are not using for school or other activities and fill it with anything you think kids might enjoy. Do you have a favorite game or hobby you'd like to share? Bring it along! The children will be excited to see whatever you bring because it is new to them.  Other items you will want in your backpack are a first-aid kit and a flashlight to help in case of an emergency. Parents will be impressed with your initiative, kids will be happy for new activities and you will be a successful babysitter when you carry the Babysitter's Backpack. Here are some suggestions for your pack:

- ◎ Bible
- ◎ *The Official Christian Babysitting Guide*
- ◎ Videos
- ◎ Yo-yo
- ◎ Card game
- ◎ Paper, colored pencils and crayons
- ◎ Small, travel-size versions of popular games, like checkers
- ◎ Candy (get parents' permission before giving candy to kids)
- ◎ Children's Bible or Bible story book
- ◎ Boo-Boo Repair Kit (see page 43)
- ◎ Small flashlight and extra batteries
- ◎ Film canister filled with pennies (do not use with babies)
- ◎ Bubble Magic (see instructions on page 105)
- ◎ Balloons (keep deflated ones away from babies)
- ◎ Art supplies (safety scissors, fabric, socks, glue, yarn, etc.)
- ◎ Special supplies for some activities, if needed

After each job, be sure to restock used items from your Babysitter's Backpack so you will be ready for your next job.

READY,
SET,
GO!

BEFORE YOU HEAD OUT THE DOOR, spend time with God. This time with Him will give you the strength you need to do a great job. Not only will He refresh you, you can use this time to ask Him how to best minister to the children you will babysit.

I have put my trust in you. Show me the way I should go.

~ *Psalm 143:8*

Arrive at your job early so you will have time to ask the parents questions about where things are in their home. Pull out the *Getting to Know You* form on pages 237-243 so you do not forget anything. Ask a parent to show you around the house, pointing out the fire escape routes, the location of the fire extinguishers, doors that need to be locked, etc. Ask how to use the alarm system or how to do anything unique to their home, such as securing a tricky lock. During your tour, make mental notes of any safety hazards or accidents waiting to happen, such as dangling electric cords or toys left on stairways.

Ask lots of questions! Parents will appreciate your effort to be thorough and do a good job caring for their precious children. If you haven't already, fill out the *Important Phone Numbers* form on page 245 with essential information such as emergency phone numbers, where the parents can be reached and the phone number of a nearby neighbor or relative who can be called for help if necessary. You also may want to have the parents fill out the

Medical Treatment Consent Form on page 247 in case medical attention is necessary and the parents cannot be reached. Having this information on hand will give you the confidence you need to respond quickly in an emergency or contact the parents while they are away. You only need to fill in this information once for each family, then keep it to use the next time you babysit for them.

Discuss feeding, bathing and sleeping arrangements for the children. Ask what and when the children are allowed to eat and drink, as well as bedtimes. Does baby Beth sleep with a pacifier? Is little Matthew used to having a story read to him at bedtime? Also find out if the children have any allergies or medical needs, where the medicine is kept and how to administer it, if necessary.

FIND IT FAST

Put your emergency phone number list near the phone. If you do have an emergency, you might not have time to search for the list.

~ALEXA, 11
SEATTLE, WA

If there is time, ask the parents which activities the children like best, and of course, what is not allowed. Find out about rooms that are off-limits or if TV-watching is permitted or limited. Respect and follow the family's house rules, even if they are different from your own. When the children realize that you know their parents' rules, you can avoid the "Mom lets us" excuse.

I am with you and will watch over you wherever you go.
~ *Genesis 28:15*

HOME SAFE HOME QUIZ

Need some practice preparing for safety? Find and circle all of the potential hazards in this picture. Then when you get to your job, look for the same hazards (and others) so you can prevent accidents or injuries. The answers are on the next page.

ANSWERS TO THE "HOME SAFE HOME QUIZ":

Bedroom
◎ Closet door open. Clutter and boxes that could be pulled over.
◎ Breakable items on dresser.
◎ Fan on the floor.

Stairs
◎ Use a gate at the stairs.
◎ Ball left on stairs.
◎ No handrail.

Kitchen
◎ Electrical appliances within reach.
◎ Pet food dishes on the floor that could be a temptation to a baby.
◎ Long knives left on the counter.
◎ Pots with handles turned out.
◎ Bug spray and cleaners under the counter with doors open.
◎ Trash can without a lid.

Living Room
◎ An open fireplace, matches nearby.
◎ Electric cords dangling beside table within a baby's reach.
◎ Loose area rug tangled up.
◎ Electrical outlets without safety covers, with a screwdriver laying next to it.
◎ Dangling drapery within baby's reach.
◎ Window open.
◎ Furniture with sharp edges.

Bathroom
◎ Open medicine cabinet for curious hands and mouths.
◎ Toilet seat left up.
◎ Cleaners on the floor next to the toilet.
◎ Bathtub filled with water.
◎ Blow dryer plugged in, left on counter.

DON'T LEAVE, mommy!

WHEN IT IS YOUR FIRST TIME BABYSITTING for a family, sit down and become acquainted with the children while the parents are still home. Children need time to get to know you, too.

They are more comfortable tackling this transition while their parents are still there. This is especially true if you are babysitting a toddler who doesn't want Mommy and Daddy to leave. As the parents prepare to go, get the children involved in games or other activities to focus their minds on having fun rather than being "abandoned." Then the parents can slip out the door, unnoticed.

When you arrive just on time or even late, parents may feel uneasy and be in a rush to get out the door. If parents are concerned about getting to a restaurant in time for a reservation or catching a movie before it starts, they won't be able to help you through this critical transition time. Suddenly, you're stuck listening to 2-year-old Dylan scream while he clutches the front-door knob for the next hour. Try to arrive early or at least on time.

When a child is upset about his or her parents leaving, explain what time they will be back in a way kids understand. Say something like, "They'll be back right after Sesame Street" instead of just "3:30." Never lie to the child about when the parents will be back. Instead, acknowledge the child and reassure him that everything will be

TERRIFIC TIP!

SCREAM SAVER

Quiet crying kids by slipping in one of their family's vacation or holiday videos. Seeing their parents, even if it is just on TV, will comfort kids. But be sure to get permission from the parents before you use the videos.

~MARY, 13
COLUMBUS, OH

WAAAAAAAAAA! • WAAAAAAAAAA! • WAAAAAAAAAA! • WAAAAAAAAAA! • WAAAAAAAAAA! • WAAAAAAAAAA!

okay, give the child a hug and move on to another activity. Ask to see the child's room, take a walk if it's daytime or offer to play a game. Most kids will quickly brighten as they start having fun!

PRAYER FOR PROTECTION

Dear God, You are my helper. When I am scared, I can call on Your name because You will never leave me. Thank You for Your angels that watch over me. In Jesus' name, Amen.

AFTER THE PARENTS LEAVE

✓ Pray to God for safety and protection.

✓ Turn on the porch light if it is dark outside.

✓ Make sure all windows and doors are locked.

✓ Every 15 minutes, check on children who are sleeping.

✓ Help children with homework and chores.

✓ Organize games and other activities to keep kids occupied.

A WORD on THE WAY

When I am afraid, I will trust in you. In God, whose word I praise, in God I trust; I will not be afraid.

~ *Psalm 56:3-4*

SAFETY FIRST

TENDERLY CARING FOR CHILDREN when they are injured or sick is an important part of your job. In fact, Jesus said healing is "the work of him [God] who sent me" (John 9:4). When you are bandaging a cut or removing a stinger, remember that you are doing God's work.

TAKE A CLASS

This section is not a first-aid manual but it is full of hints and tips to help you. Check with your local American Red Cross chapter or a nearby children's hospital for courses in babysitting and first-aid. Even if you are a veteran babysitter, it never hurts to take a refresher course in basic first-aid. If you get your first-aid certification, you will be in even more demand and you will feel prepared for any emergency.

BOO-BOO REPAIR KIT

Have a Boo-Boo Repair Kit (a first-aid kit) on hand, ready for an emergency. When you put your kit together, make sure you have all the supplies listed below. Have your kit complete so you can confidently head off to a job on a moment's notice. Store your Boo-Boo Repair Kit in your Babysitter Backpack to make sure you don't forget it!

Your Boo-Boo Repair Kit should have the following supplies:

◉ fun, colorful bandages in different shapes and sizes

◉ disposable gloves (at least two pairs)

◉ tweezers (to remove splinters)

◉ hand wipes or hand cleaner

- gauze pads
- roll of gauze bandage
- blunt scissors
- pen and paper
- cold pack
- zip-style storage bag

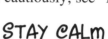

- bottle of ipecac (use cautiously; see "Poison" on page 46)

(use cautiously; see "Poison" on page 46)

OUCH!

OUCH!

STAY CALM

During an emergency, there is no need to panic. Remember, you're not alone. God is your helper and He is with you! When you need to remember how to do something or even what to do, He will guide you. John 14:26 says, "But the Counselor, the Holy Spirit, whom the Father will send in my name, will teach you all things and will remind you of everything I have said to you."

TERRIFIC TIP!

The Lord has put you in charge now, and He knows you can handle it. The children are relying on you, too, so take a deep breath and remember Jesus' words: "Peace I leave with you; my peace I give you. I do not give to you as the world gives. Do not let your hearts be troubled and do not be afraid" (John 14:27).

GLOVE GUARDS

It's good to have some disposable gloves with you for changing diapers or if you have to clean up urine or vomit. They will keep you from spreading any sickness and from getting sick yourself.

~MALEAH, 12
TAMPA, FL

GET HELP

When it's a real emergency, like a fire or a possible intruder, call 9-1-1 for help. Once you and the children are out of danger, let the parents know what's going on. Don't be afraid to call for help even when you are not sure if you need it. It is always better to be safe than sorry.

FiRE

Don't try to put out the flames yourself. Yell "Fire" as loud as possible. Close the door to the room where the fire is, if possible. Get the children out of the house and do not go back for any reason. Take the children to a neighbor's house and call 9-1-1. Then call the parents to let them know.

MAKE A SAFE GETAWAY

During a fire, smoke rises while clean air stays near the floor. To escape, get down on your knees and crawl to an exit. Tell the children to crawl behind you. Follow the family's fire escape plan for finding the closest exit, if they have one.

iF YOU CATCH On FiRE

If your clothing catches on fire, remember: stop, drop and roll. First, stop dead in your tracks and don't panic. Running only fans the flames and makes them more intense. Next, drop to the floor, covering your face with your hands. Roll over and over to smother the flames. Fire needs oxygen to burn, so rolling on top of the fire puts it out. If one of the children's clothes catches fire, help them stop, drop and roll in a blanket or rug if one is nearby.

BURnS

The best first-aid for burns is to run cool water over the burned area for 10 minutes. Do not bandage the burn or put any kind of ointment on it. If the burn starts to blister, call 9-1-1 immediately.

Poison

If you find a child playing with medicine and believe the child has swallowed it (an open bottle is a good clue that something is wrong), call the Poison Control Center. If you don't have the number, call 9-1-1. Have the medicine bottle with you when you call. Tell the poison control counselor the name of the product and the amount you believe the child swallowed. You may be asked to give the child milk or a dose of syrup of ipecac, which causes the medicine to be vomited. Carefully follow the Poison Control Center's instructions. Never give any medication to a child without instructions from someone at the Poison Control Center. Families usually keep syrup of ipecac in the medicine cabinet. You could also keep a bottle in your Boo-Boo Repair Kit.

TERRIFIC TIP!

Poison Symptoms

If kids have any of these symptoms, they might be poisoned: stomach cramps, vomiting, burns around their mouth, sudden change in the way they act or convulsions. You should call the Poison Control Center or 9-1-1 immediately. It's better to be safe than sorry!

~Emma, 11
SAVANNAH, GA

Nicks and Bruises

Skinned knees and small cuts can hurt! Lightly touch the area using a soft, clean cloth or towel to stop the bleeding. Then gently wash the area with soap and water. Apply a colorful bandage from your Boo-Boo repair kit. Comfort and reassure the child that everything is going to be okay.

Gushing Blood

For heavy bleeding, place a clean cloth over the wound and apply pressure. Raise the area higher than the heart to help slow the bleeding. Call 9-1-1 immediately if the blood is spurting.

OUCH!

OUCH!

FEVER

If the child feels hot to you, take the child's temperature to check for a fever. If the child has a fever, call the parents. Offer the child a drink of cool water while you wait for the parents to arrive. Comfort the child by praying for him or her.

NOSE BLEED

Have the child lean slightly forward while you pinch closed his or her nostrils for 5 minutes. Wrap ice in a washcloth and apply it to the bridge of the child's nose to help stop the bleeding.

INSECT STINGS AND BITES

To remove the stinger, scrape it out with your fingernail or a playing card. Wash bug bites and stings with soap and water. Apply an ice pack (ice in a resealable bag will work) to the bite or sting to reduce swelling and pain.

An allergic reaction to a bug bite can be life-threatening. Symptoms may include: swelling of the eyes, lips or tongue; coughing or wheezing; stomach cramps; vomiting; difficulty breathing or dizziness. If a child has one or more of these symptoms after an insect bite, call 9-1-1 immediately.

TERRIFIC TIP!

SPONGE SOOTHER

Here is an easy way to make boo-boos feel better. Cut a clean sponge into several small pieces (about 1" x 2" each). Dip the sponge pieces in water and put them in resealable plastic bags. Put the bags in the freezer until one is needed. The sponges are small enough for even little kids to hold!

~TESS, 12
LANCASTER, PA

OUCH!

OUCH!

CHOKING

If the child can't cough, speak or is not breathing, you must act immediately. Help the child first, then call 9-1-1. If someone is with you, ask them to call 9-1-1 while you help the child.

OUCH!

FOR A CHILD OVER A YEAR OLD

1. Stand behind the child and wrap your arms around his or her waist.

OUCH!

2. Press your fist in between the rib cage and belly button. Grab your fist with the other hand and push upward and inward to dislodge the object.

3. Continue to repeat until the child spits out whatever he or she was choking on and starts to breathe.

4. Call 9-1-1 and then the parents.

FOR BABIES

1. While sitting, turn the baby over on his tummy. Straddle the baby's face along your arm. Support his head and jaw with your hand, keeping the baby's head lower than his body.

2. Rest your arm on your thigh, and using the heel of your hand, give five forceful blows between the baby's shoulder blades.

3. Gently turn over the baby while continuing to support the baby's head. Place three fingers over the breastbone, between the nipples.

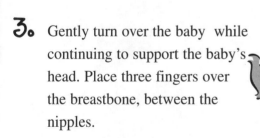

4. Press firmly with your middle and ring fingers four times. Repeat steps 2, 3 and 4 until the object comes out.

5. Call 9-1-1 and then the parents.

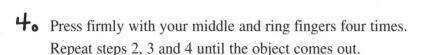
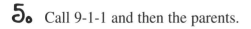

BABYSITTER DO'S AND DON'TS

◎ **DON'T** leave the children alone in the house, even for a moment.

◎ **DO** take the children with you if you must leave in an emergency situation.

◎ **DON'T** open the door to strangers.

◎ **DO** keep the doors and windows locked at all times and turn on an outside light after dark.

◎ **DON'T** go outside to investigate any unusual noises.

◎ **DO** call the parents or police if you are seriously concerned.

◎ **DON'T** tie up the phone.

◎ **DO** call for help, if you need it.

◎ **DO** respect the privacy of others.

OUCH!

OUCH!

- ◎ **DON'T** poke and snoop around.

- ◎ **DON'T** invite friends in the house, unless the parents have agreed to it.

- ◎ **DO** bring things to do after the kids have fallen asleep, like homework or a craft.

- ◎ **DON'T** fall asleep.

- ◎ **DO** keep television, radio and stereo volumes down low so you can hear if the baby cries or any other unusual noises.

- ◎ **DON'T** give any medication to a child unless the parents have asked you to do so.

- ◎ **DO** call a parent if a child becomes ill or gets injured.

OUCH!

OUCH!

∞ • ∞ ♥ ∞ ♥ ∞ • ∞

TELEPHONE ETIQUETTE

HOW TO ANSWER THE PHONE

Never tell a caller that you are a babysitter alone with the children. Just say, "Mrs. Johnson is unavailable to come to the phone right now. Can I take a message for her?" Be sure to write down the full message left by the caller. Note all calls on the *Babysitter's Report* on page 251. Note the time of the call, the caller's name and phone number, and any messages.

IS IT OKAY TO MAKE A PHONE CALL?

Parents don't usually mind if you need to make a quick call to verify travel arrangements home or to check with a friend about tomorrow's homework assignment. But calls should be kept to a minimum. Remember, you are there to watch the children, not to catch up on the latest gossip! If you keep the phone line busy, you may miss an important phone call from the parents.

WHEN TO CALL 9-1-1

In an emergency, you need to act fast. Don't hesitate to call for help when someone is seriously injured or ill. In life-threatening situations, medical care is needed right away. Call 9-1-1 or another local emergency number if the child:

◎ Has trouble breathing or stops breathing
◎ Is choking uncontrollably
◎ Is bleeding and you can't get it to stop
◎ Is unable to move his legs or arms
◎ Has a broken bone
◎ Is unconscious
◎ Has no heartbeat (or pulse)

WHAT TO SAY WHEN CALLING 9-1-1

1. Tell your name and that you are the babysitter.

2. Tell the dispatcher what the emergency is. If anyone is injured and needs help, let them know that. Follow any instructions they may give you. For example, you might say: "A 5-year-old child I am babysitting for fell off the swing and her arm looks broken."

3. Give the address of the house where you are calling from and the nearest cross street. This is information you should have on the *Getting to Know You* form.

4. Give the phone number from where you are calling.

5. Don't hang up until the dispatcher tells you to hang up. The dispatcher may have instructions for you to follow until help arrives.

I will help you speak and
will teach you what
to say.

~ *Exodus 4:12*

BUT mom LETS US!

SOME KIDS WILL TAKE ADVANTAGE of mom and dad's absence to try out their new skates on the dining room table — or any other activity they know they cannot do when their parents are home. Of course, you will have to stop them before they hurt themselves or wreck the entire house. It's up to you to maintain law and order. That is what the parents have hired you to do.

Let the children know what is coming next as you move from activity to activity. Say something like, "When you finish taking your bath, I will read you a story." This will make the transition to the next activity easier and will help the child not to dawdle. A gentle reminder like "It's 7:00 now, and you know that you go to bed at 7:30, so we can only play one more game" will help the child be more conscious of time and not so surprised when you announce bedtime.

Offer the child choices for ways to accomplish an activity. This will encourage him to cooperate with you and make him feel more independent. For example, instead of saying, "Time to clean up!" ask, "Would you like to put away the crayons and coloring books or put the trucks and cars in the toy box?"

To make mealtimes go more smoothly, instead of saying, "You have to eat the vegetables I made!" try explaining, "We can have green beans or sweet corn. Which one would you like to have?"

Choices for young children should be simple ones like "Do you want to wear your purple pajamas or the green ones?" But be

TERRIFIC TIP!

TIMER TAMER

Keep kids from fighting over a toy by setting a timer for a certain amount of time. When the buzzer rings, it is the next kid's turn to play with the toy.

~JASMINE, 12
KANSAS CITY, MO

careful about giving choices. Some rules are not negotiable, such as bedtimes.

So what do you do when you tell a kid he can't do something and he shouts, "Mom lets us!"?

When a child is angry because he can't have his own way, it is up to you to stay cool. Your calmness will help him settle down. If you angrily scold him, he will see what a powerful effect his words and actions have on you and he will be more likely to continue throwing a tantrum. Instead, focus on the emotion behind the child's words. Say, "I can see you're upset because you can't use your skates in the house. I'll check with your mom and see if it's okay to do it the next time I'm here." That kind of response shows him that you understand his frustration and will be informing his  parents of the incident. Keep anger resolution to three steps: acknowledge feelings, make rules clear and stand firm.

Here are six situations where the three steps can be applied:

STICKY SITUATION 1

The child wants to eat a lollipop before dinner. You do not allow her to do so. She screams, "I hate you" because she doesn't get her way.

Acknowledge her feelings:

"I understand you are angry because you can't have your lollipop right now."

Make the rules clear:

"Your words hurt my feelings. We should not say things that hurt other people's feelings."

Stand firm:

"Candy must wait until after dinner."

STICKY SITUATION 2

The child doesn't want to got to bed. Instead, he kicks and screams.

Acknowledge his feelings:

"You're upset that it is time for bed."

Make the rules clear:

"It is okay to be disappointed that it is time to go to bed, but not to throw a tantrum."

Stand firm:

"Time to get your pajamas on, Jude."

STICKY SITUATION 3

The child comes running to you to complain that his sister is cheating at a game.

Acknowledge her feelings:

"You're right. She shouldn't do that, but that is something you should work out with her."

Make the rules clear:

"Tell her you don't like it when she cheats."

Stand firm:

Encourage the children to first try settling the squabbles on their own before reporting them to you.

STICKY SITUATION 4

The child blames her imaginary playmate, George, for the spilled milk on the kitchen floor.

Acknowledge her feelings:

"Sometimes we need to be more careful."

Make the rules clear:

"You are responsible for your friend George. You need to tell him to be more careful."

Stand firm:

Respect the child's imagination, but affirm that rules still apply.

STiCKY SiTUATiON 5

An older child says, "I already washed my hands" when you know he did not.

Acknowledge his feelings:

"I know you don't like washing your hands, but you still need to do it."

Make the rules clear:

"We need to wash our hands before we eat to stay healthy."

Stand firm:

"Please go wash your hands now."

STiCKY SiTUATiON 6

The parents asked you to make sure the kids do their homework before playing. The kids say it is already done but you know they did not finish it.

Acknowledge the kids' feelings:

"I know homework is not as fun as playing outside."

Make the rules clear:

"The sooner you get your homework done the sooner you can go play."

Stand firm:

"Let's go over your homework together."

Make sure that nobody pays back wrong for wrong, but always try to be kind to each other and to everyone else.

~ 1 Thessalonians 5:15

STiCKS AND STONES MAY BREAK MY BONES...

When children say mean things to you, a sibling or a friend, it is a good opportunity to share about a better way for them to behave. The Bible says in 1 Thessalonians 5:13 to "live in peace with each other." Remind the children that calling someone a name never solves anything. Try sharing the following story about what happened to King David in 2 Samuel 16:5-14.

STiCKS AND STONES (2 SAMUEL 16:5-14)

Ask, "Have you ever heard the saying 'Sticks and stones may break my bones, but words will never hurt me'?" Allow the children to respond. Say, "It isn't true, is it? Words really do hurt, especially when someone calls you a name. There's a story in the Bible about a man named Shimei who called King David bad names and even threw stones at him. That wasn't a nice thing to do, was it?" Allow the children to answer. Ask, "Do you know what King David did?" Let the children try to guess. Ask, "Do you think he told his soldiers to kill Shimei? Do you think he called Shimei names and threw stones back at him? No, David told his friends to pay no attention to Shimei. David said God would hear and repay good to David for all the bad things Shimei said. So the next time someone calls you a name, think about doing what King David did."

iT'S A WAR

As you know, brothers and sisters sometimes fight. Sibling fighting may be only with words, other times they may scratch, kick and claw to get what they want. If the fighting ever gets physical, jump in and stop them! You don't want the parents to come home to bruised and battered kids.

THE BEST WAY TO END A FIGHT:

1. Give each child a time-out and ask each child to go sit quietly in different rooms to settle down.

2. Speak to each child alone about why their were fighting. You may already know, but this will help the child to air his or her feelings.

3. Bring both children together to brainstorm how the problem can be peacefully resolved. Lead the discussion and do not allow it to turn ugly again. Hopefully, you will be able to help the children find a compromise.

4. Lead the children through the forgiveness process by asking each one to say, "I'm sorry" or "Will you forgive me?" to each other. This is an important step that shouldn't be ignored! Then ask the children if you can pray with them to ask God to help them be friends. If the children want to pray themselves, let them. You can ask them to pray for each other if you sense they will, otherwise don't push it. Even if you can only get them to sit down and talk, your efforts will be successful!

5. Let the parents know what happened and how you resolved it. Ask them if they would prefer you handle arguments in a different way next time.

WHEN IT'S NOT TATTLING

It can be easy to tune out tattling kids, but sometimes the tattling can mean there is a real problem. Always listen carefully to what the children are saying. Let them know it's okay to tell you if they are being physically hurt by another child or if there is a dangerous activity going on, like playing with matches.

REWARDING GOOD BEHAVIOR

When you compliment a child for her good behavior, the positive feedback will encourage the child to repeat that behavior. One way you can reinforce good behavior is by saying something like, "I'm proud of you for picking up all the blocks off the floor. God is pleased, too." This will make the child feel good about her accomplishment.

Another way you can show the child you appreciate her help is to offer a reward, like a sticker or small treat. You will be creating a pleasurable babysitting experience for you and them!

TERRIFIC TIP!

no CHOKE!

Don't reward small kids with hard candy. They can choke on it.

~CAROLINE , 13
BOZEMAN, MT

PLAY WITH MEEEEEEEEE!

When more than one child is fighting for your attention, choose a game or craft in which everyone can be involved. Tell the children, "We can all play!" Even when one child is a toddler and the sibling is older, both can enjoy the special attention you give by choosing a game or craft that is suitable for the youngest child. The older child may complain a bit, but explain, "Let's do this one for Susie. Then you can pick the next game." Or, if the younger child goes to bed earlier, say, "Let's do this now, then when Susie goes to bed we can play the game you like."

But MOM lets us! • But MOM lets us! • But MOM lets us! • But MOM lets us! • But MOM lets us! • But MOM lets us!

But MOM lets us! • But MOM lets us! • But MOM lets us! • But MOM lets us! • But MOM lets us! • But MOM lets us!

THEIR SPACE

If an older child wants to be alone, let him. Just peek in on him every 15-20 minutes or so to make sure everything is okay. Remember, you are "invading" his space, so respect his privacy and knock on the door before entering. Let him know you are nearby if he needs anything.

PRAYER FOR GOD'S HELP

Dear God, thank You for the chance to babysit (name of children). I commit this time to You, Lord, and I know that all my plans will succeed. I am Your disciple, taught of the Lord, and I will teach these children as You have taught me. Give us peace and safety. In Jesus' name, Amen.

Cast all your anxiety on him because he cares for you.
~ 1 Peter 5:7

THE SCOOP
on POOP

THE SCOOP ON POOP IS THIS: Diapers are a major part of a baby's life until potty training, which is usually around ages 2-3 (some kids start earlier and some start later). A happy baby is a baby with a clean diaper. After all, how would you like to sit around in a soiled diaper and not be able to change it? When a baby cries, it is often to let you know that she wants a clean diaper. But some children will not cry for a diaper change, so it's up to you to check the diaper from time to time. A dirty diaper left on too long can cause diaper rash, which feels like a bad sunburn.

HOW TO CHANGE A DIAPER

1. Place the baby in a safe place, like a playpen or crib.

2. Gather all of the supplies you will need: a clean diaper (two if it is a boy baby), baby wipes, a small toy and an extra change of clothes in case of a mess. If possible, wear disposable gloves to change diapers.

3. With one hand supporting the back of the baby's head and the other around her body, gently lay the baby on the changing table.

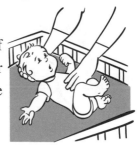

4. Give the baby a toy to play with as a distraction while you work. Keeping her busy will help her from getting her hands and feet in your way.

5. Carefully remove her clothing, keeping one hand on her so she doesn't fall off the table.

6. Unfasten the dirty diaper. Gently lift the baby by grasping her ankles with one hand. Quickly remove the dirty diaper, wad it up and retape the tabs tightly so the mess won't fall out. Set the dirty diaper aside to throw away when you are finished. For a boy, lay a clean diaper over his penis to prevent a stream of urine in your face!

7. Thoroughly clean the baby's bottom and genitals with a baby wipe, wiping from front to back and paying close attention to all the hidden crevices. Be careful—if you rub a wipe with poop on the genital area the baby could get an infection. Use

ointment on diaper rashes if the parents instructed you to do so.

8. Unfold a new diaper and slide it under the baby's bottom with the tabs in back. Align the top of the diaper with the baby's waist. Pull the clean diaper between her legs and tuck it around her tummy. Fasten the tabs firmly over the front. The diaper should fit snugly so it won't fall off but not so tightly that it cuts off circulation in her legs or waist.

9. If the baby's pants were dirty, dress her in a clean pair after changing the diaper. Move the baby from the changing table to a safe place while you dispose of the diaper and wash your hands.

POTTY TRAINERS

Patience is the key when dealing with children who are just learning to use the toilet. It is common for children who have learned to use the potty to accidentally wet or soil their pants. Just stay calm. Reassure the child that it is "just an accident," take him to the bathroom and help him clean up. Don't scold or fuss at a child who has an accident! This will only make the child feel badly and it won't help the child remember to use the toilet the next time. Be sure to let the parents know about any potty accidents or successes when they return home. They will want to know everything that happened.

TERRIFIC TIP!

BUSY BUBBLES

Have a jar of bubbles nearby when you change a baby's diaper. If the baby is moving around too much, blow some bubbles. The bubbles will distract the baby while you get the diaper changed.

~JENNA, 12
COLORADO SPRINGS, CO

Ask a potty-trainer every 30 minutes or so if she needs to "go." If she says no with her words but is dancing around in a way that means she obviously needs to go, gently take her hand and say in a cheery voice, "Come on, let's go to the potty. I'll read you a story while you sit." If this or nothing else works, then wait patiently until she is ready to go. You cannot make her do it!

Ask the parents for tips on encouraging the child to use the potty. Some families have a chart system or offer a "treat" when the child uses the potty correctly.

A POTTY ROUTINE

If you have a potty-trainer, incorporate potty times into the schedule. For example, after you come inside from playing, tell everyone to go to the potty and wash their hands. Also remind the children to take a bathroom break and wash their hands before and after meals and while getting ready for bed. Even older children need a little potty motivation at times!

At naptime and bedtime, a potty-trainer may wear a diaper. Be sure to ask the parents about this so you will know how to handle the situation. If the child does not wear a diaper, ask her to sit on the potty before going to bed. Remind the child to get up or call for you if she feels the need to go!

A WORD ON THE WAY

I lift up my eyes to the hills – where does my help come from? My help comes from the Lord, the Maker of heaven and earth.

~ Psalm 121:1-2

SPLISH SPLASH!

DO NOT BATHE A BABY unless the parents have asked you to and you feel comfortable with it. You may want to ask the parents if you can watch them bathe the baby first. That way you'll feel more confident and relaxed when you get the opportunity to do it.

HOW TO BATHE A BABY

1. Place the baby in a crib or playpen while you gather everything you need.

 2. Gather everything you need: tear-free shampoo, towel, soap, toys, washcloth, diaper and clothes.

3. Fill the baby bathtub with a few inches of water. Test the water temperature with your elbow.

4. Gently undress the baby and place him in the tub.

5. Keep one hand on the baby at all times. Using your free hand, gently soap him.

 6. Using only a few drops of shampoo, gently rub the baby's hair. Rinse well by pouring cups of warm water over his head.

7. Drape a towel over your shoulder and carefully lift the baby out of the water. Wrap the towel around the baby quickly so he won't get chilled. Dry the baby, making sure to wipe all of his crevices. Diaper and dress the baby.

GIVING A BATH

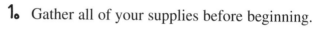

Giving a small child a bath can be like trying to hold on to a slippery fish, so be careful! If giving a bath is something new for you and you would prefer not to do it, let the parents know. They may instead ask you give the child a "bird bath" (see page 77).

If you do feel comfortable giving a child a bath, don't forget to:

1. Gather all of your supplies before beginning.

2. Test the water temperature by dipping your elbow in the water.

3. Fill the tub with 4-6 inches of warm (not hot) water.

4. Keep one hand on the child at all times while washing and rinsing.

5. Help the child out of the tub. Towel-dry them completely before dressing them in pajamas.

OLDER KIDS

If a child is old enough to bathe himself, give him the privacy to do so. Stay close by, though, in case you need to get to him quickly. Leave the bathroom door slightly cracked open if you suspect the child might need you.

TERRIFIC TIP!

SLIPPER STOPPERS

When you are giving a small kid a bath, have them wear their aqua socks if they have them. The rubber grips will keep them from falling in the tub.

~SAMANTHA, 11
SALEM, OR

WHAT'S A BIRD BATH?

Imagine a bird landing in your bathroom sink and splashing around. Now instead of a bird, imagine it's a child doing the splashing. This kind of bath may not be quite as fun for the child as taking a regular bath, but it's safer and easier for you.

Seat the child on the counter next to the sink or have him stand next to you. Use a cloth to wipe him off. If the child is old enough (about 4 years old), allow him to wash his own face and hands. If he is too short to reach the sink, get a stool for him to stand on. Kids at that age love to be independent. Of course, you might still need to help him wash the spots he misses!

TERRIFIC TIP!

1. Fill the bathroom sink with warm water.

2. Use a clean, wet washcloth or sponge to clean the child's face, neck, ears and so on.

3. Don't forget the soap!

SHAVE SAVE

For little boys who hate to have their faces washed, try spreading a little shaving cream on their face with the soap, then "shave" it off with the flat side of a comb.

~ASHLEY, 11
RICHMOND, KY

A WORD ON THE WAY

Wash away all my iniquity and cleanse me from my sin.

~ *Psalm 51:2*

TiME FOR BED

BABiES AND TODDLERS

Before the parents leave, find out if the baby or toddler sleeps with a pacifier or has a favorite blanket. Otherwise, at bedtime the toddler may scream for "inky" or "hanky" and you won't know what he or she is talking about! Write this information on the *Getting to Know You* form on pages 237-243.

Babies may need your help falling asleep. Going from blaring lights and television to total darkness in 60 seconds won't work! Babies need time to wind down, too. Try playing soft, soothing music as you get the baby ready for bed. Make sure the baby has a fresh, dry diaper to wear to bed and is dressed in cozy pajamas that are warm or cool enough for the weather.

Talk softly and tell her, "It's time for bed." Spend a few minutes cuddling and rocking her gently back and forth as you carry her to her crib. Lay her down slowly, patting her lightly. Cover her with her blanket. Babies less than 1 year old should be placed on their sides to sleep.

Switch on the nightlight if one is used and quietly close the door. Peek in on her after 10 or 15 minutes to make sure she's okay.

Babies will sometimes fuss a bit before falling to sleep. Other times, they may cry to let you know something is wrong. If crying continues more than 5 minutes (which will feel like an eternity to you!), go in and check on her.

WAHHHHH!

Before digging your nails into the ceiling from frazzled nerves, remember crying is the only way babies can communicate they need something.

CRYING BABY CHECKLIST

✓ Is the baby wearing a dirty diaper?

✓ Is the baby hungry?

✓ Did you try rocking her?

✓ Is the baby tired and ready to go to sleep?

✓ Is the baby hot or cold?

✓ Does the baby have gas and need to be burped?

✓ Has the baby lost her pacifier or favorite blanket?

✓ Have you tried winding up a musical mobile or playing soft music?

✓ Have you tried turning the lights low and walking with the baby in your arms?

TERRIFIC TIP!

NEEDED: mommy!

When you have tried everything you can think of and the baby is still crying, call the parents. The baby may be sick.

~BRIANNE, 13
NASHVILLE, TN

OLDER CHILDREN

It's 6:00 — time to get the kids ready for bed! Well, okay, maybe it's not time for them to actually go to bed, but smart babysitters know that an early effort will make bedtime easier for everyone. There are ways to help the children feel sleepy and ready to go to bed when it is time. Try this routine:

1. Play with the child or children — something that involves lots of activity. Your goal is to wear them out! If it is light outside, have fun with the kids running around the yard. Kids will burn up energy playing Prayer Tag, Pharaoh's Frogs or  another outdoor game from the *Playtime* section starting on page

95. If it's dark and the parents prefer that you stay inside, play an indoor game such as The Widow's Penny or another indoor game from the *Playtime* section. After the game or activity, tell the children it's time to clean up the toys. Motivate them by telling them that once they are finished, they will get a snack.

2. After all the fun, the kids may be hungry. Have them wash their hands, then serve a good evening snack like Tower of Babel Stacks (page 210) or Ants on a Log (page 197). Full tummies will help the kids begin to feel sleepy.

3. What's more relaxing than a nice, warm bath? Make this a calm, relaxing time, not a water-pistol shoot off. You don't want the kids to get recharged like it's time to go play again. You may want to use this time to tell a Bible story about water, such as Jesus walking on water, how Jesus calmed the storm or how Paul got shipwrecked. Use bath toys as props and let the children get involved by role playing.

TERRIFIC TIP!

SING 'N' SOAP

To make sure the kids wash their hands for a long enough time, have them sing "Happy Birthday to You" while they are washing.

~ALLISON, 12
PASADENA, CA

4. Get the children ready for bed by helping them change into their pajamas, get drinks of water and make potty visits.

5. Have a quiet time to soothe the children. The kids should now be beginning to settle down. Turn off the TV and any other noisy distractions. Dim the bedroom lights if possible and play soothing music, like a quiet worship tape. Ask the children to climb into bed so you can read them a story. For very young children who can't sit still for a story, ask the toddler to point to things in the picture like Jesus or the cross.

6. After reading a story, ask the children if they would like to pray. If the children are hesitant about praying aloud, ask if you can say a prayer for them. Here is a short prayer to comfort little sleepyheads:

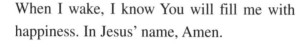

PRAYER FOR BEDTIME

Dear God, I will lie down and sleep in peace because You keep me safe. As I sleep, I will not be afraid because Your angels watch over me. When I wake, I know You will fill me with happiness. In Jesus' name, Amen.

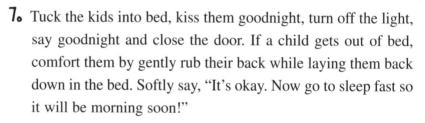

7. Tuck the kids into bed, kiss them goodnight, turn off the light, say goodnight and close the door. If a child gets out of bed, comfort them by gently rub their back while laying them back down in the bed. Softly say, "It's okay. Now go to sleep fast so it will be morning soon!"

8. Check on the child or children every half-hour.

⋯⋯⋯⋯⋯⋯⋯⋯⋯⋯⋯⋯⋯⋯⋯⋯⋯⋯⋯⋯⋯

The Lord is my helper; I will not be afraid.
~ Hebrews 13:6

BABYSITTING WITH A PURPOSE

INSTEAD OF JUST OCCUPYING THE CHILDREN until their parents return, make your time with them productive. That's what *The Official Christian Babysitting Guide* is all about! Your

job has purpose and meaning. You are not there by accident; you have been chosen by God to oversee and care for these children while the parents are away. What an awesome responsibility!

Grab the kids' interest by using a theme. Starting on page 91 are a bunch of themes geared toward helping children become excited about God and the Bible. You will notice that each theme has its own picture icon. Once you select a theme, look for that icon throughout the rest of this book to find games, activities, crafts and snacks that can be matched with that theme. Decide which parts you want to use by what fits your needs and your babysitting schedule. You can even mix-and-match from the themes!

Feeling creative? Why not design your own theme around a favorite Bible story? Find a craft, game and snack that present your story in a concrete way. Kids learn best when the main ideas involve all senses: sight, sound, touch, taste and smell. Keep in mind the children's age levels and what they can do at those levels. For instance, some games are not suitable for preschoolers who cannot read. There is nothing more frustrating for a child than the feeling that they are not able to do something that looks fun!

KIDS LOVE BOOKS

Children are never too young or old to enjoy your reading to them. Books open up a window to the world that no one can close. Any Christian books you choose can inspire the kids to a greater appreciation for God and His creation.

As you gather materials for your theme, remember that great Bible story books and picture books spark kids' interest in God and the Bible. Look around your house for books you loved as a kid. Those you loved reading as a child will probably become favorites of theirs, too. But if searching for the right book (see "Choosing the Right Book" below) becomes time-consuming, you might want to invest in a beginner's Bible or children's devotional to use for all your themes. Pack it away in your Babysitter's Backpack so you will always be ready.

CHOOSING THE RIGHT BOOK

It is important to choose the right book for the right age. Here is a chart to help you select the appropriate book for each age:

Age	Books
Infant-2 years old	foam cushion books, board books, nursery rhymes, ABC books
2-6 years old	picture books, illustrated books, animal characters
5-8 years old	beginning readers, story books, life experiences and feelings, simple science, craft and recipe books
6-10 years old	chapter books, fiction series, fact collections, humor

READING TO INFANTS AND TODDLERS

The best books for very young children are simple picture books that focus on a simple concept, such as animals, letters or colors. While reading one of these to a child, you might want to refer to the real objects in the illustrations. For example, if you are reading an animal book, show the child the picture, then show the matching object like a toy duck or cat. This will help children build a relationship between books and their world. You don't have to spend your own money

on books like these — just go the library and check them out, or ask to borrow a book from your younger brother or sister.

READING TO OLDER CHILDREN

Colorful pictures and interesting stories will catch the children's attention, but they want to interact and be involved in the story. They don't want to simply read about Moses and the burning bush, they want to see, taste and touch it! That's why after you read the story, you should follow up with an activity and snack related to the story. The interaction of hands-on activities will seal in their mind the memory of the Bible story's message. You can also make a story come alive by having the children act out the story while you read it aloud. Or, tell the story using finger or hand puppets!

Either read the Bible stories from a Bible story book or from the Bible, whichever you think will best get the message across to the kids. Look around your house for books you loved as a kid or check with your

TERRIFIC TIP!

BE PREPARED

Always bring more craft supplies than you think you will need, in case of accidents.

~ROSA, 12
EVANSTON, IL

younger siblings to see if you can borrow their Bible picture books. For more ideas, flip to *Lights, Popcorn, Video!* on page 129.

TASTY TREATS

The children will remember the Bible stories even better when you make yummy snacks for them to eat and share. You can use the recipes found in *Munchies!* (page 197), or come up with your own. The possibilities are endless! If you plan to serve a special snack, call the parents first to get  their permission and check for any food allergies the children may have. You may want to make the snack at home before you go to your job. Or you can bring everything you need with you and let the kids help you make it!

IMPORTANT NOTE: Not all families will be open to Bible-related games and activities. Check with the parents before they leave to see if they mind your reading the children a Bible story, watching a Christian video or doing an activity you planned. Then respect their wishes. If they say no, you can let your Christian light shine in other ways by being kind, showing love and praying quietly to yourself for the family.

A WORD ON THE WAY

Let the little children come to me and do not hinder them, for the kingdom of God belongs to such as these.

~ Mark 10:14

BABYSITTER BIBLE THEMES

CREATION (Genesis 1-2:2)

◎ Games: Creation Sensation, page 106
   Let There Be Light, page 114
   Balloon Orbit, page 103
◎ Crafts: God Made Me, page 144
   I Am Thumbody, page 146
◎ Song: "This Little Light of Mine," page 180
◎ Snack: Thumbprint Cookies, page 209

NOAH AND THE ARK (Genesis 7-9:17)

◎ Game: Clouds of Rain Relay, page 105
◎ Crafts: Rainbow Mush, page 152
   Rain Clouds, page 151
◎ Song: "Arky, Arky," page 165
◎ Snack: Noah's Fruit Boat, page 203

MOSES AND THE TEN COMMANDMENTS (Exodus 20:1-17)

◎ Games: Pharaoh's Frogs, page 116
   Along The Nile Beach Party, page 102
◎ Craft: Fire on the Mountain, page 143
◎ Song: "This Is My Commandment," page 179
◎ Snack: Moses' Burning Bush, page 202

THE BATTLE AT JERICHO (Joshua 6:1-21)

◎ Game: Ha-Ha-Ha Hallelujah, page 110
◎ Craft: Walls You Can Eat, page 157
◎ Song: "What a Mighty God We Serve,"
   page 181
◎ Snack: Praying Hands Pretzels, page 211

STRONG SAMSON (Judges 15:1-17)

- ◎ Game: Strong As Samson, page 122
- ◎ Craft: Samson's Hair Flip Book, page 153
- ◎ Song: "My God Is So Great," page 176
- ◎ Snack: Weight-Lifting Snacks, page 211

SAMUEL HEARS GOD VOICE (1 Samuel 3)

- ◎ Game: Snap, Crackle Popping Bubbles, page 122
- ◎ Craft: Samuel's Nightlight, page 155
- ◎ Song: "Down in My Heart," page 168
- ◎ Snack: Samuel's Bedroll, page 208

DAVID AND GOLIATH (1 Samuel 17)

- ◎ Game: Pin the Stone on Goliath, page 117
- ◎ Craft: David's Slingshot Wheel, page 141
- ◎ Songs: "David Played," page 168
  "Only a Boy Named David," page 176
- ◎ Snack: Rock Candy, page 207

ELIJAH'S CHARIOT OF FIRE (2 Kings 2)

- ◎ Game: Prayer Tag, page 118
- ◎ Craft: Box Chariot, page 139
- ◎ Song: "Praise Him," page 178
- ◎ Snack: Elijah's Chariot Wheels, page 198

QUEEN ESTHER (Esther 2:8-18)

- ◎ Game: Hearts!, page 110
- ◎ Craft: Queen of Hearts, page 150
- ◎ Song: "Ho, Ho, Ho, Hosanna," page 171
- ◎ Snack: Queen of Hearts Cookies, page 205

THE BUSY ANTS (Proverbs 6:6-11)

- ◎ Game: Seek and Find, page 119
- ◎ Craft: Anthills in a Jar, page 137
- ◎ Song: "I'm in the Lord's Army," page 173
- ◎ Snack: Ants on a Log, page 197

JONAH AND THE WHALE (Jonah 1)

- ◎ Game: Jonah's Paper Tag, page 113
- ◎ Crafts: Ocean in a Bottle, page 149
  Jonah and the Whale Toy, page 147
- ◎ Songs: "Jonah's Song," page 175
  "Hallelujah," page 171
- ◎ Snack: Jonah's Whale of a Sandwich, page 201

JESUS' BIRTH (Luke 2:1-20)

- ◎ Game: The Invisible Gift, page 112
- ◎ Craft: Twisted Shepherd Staffs, page 156
- ◎ Song: "Happy Birthday to You"
- ◎ Snack: Baby Jesus Salad, page 198

PETER (Matthew 4:18-20; Luke 5:4-7)

- ◎ Game: Go Fish!, page 109
- ◎ Craft: Homemade Stickers, page 145
- ◎ Song: "Peter, James and John in a
  Sailboat," page 177
- ◎ Snack: Peter's Catch of the Day, page 204

THE WIDOW'S OFFERING (Mark 12:41-44)

- ◎ Game: The Widow's Penny, page 127
- ◎ Craft: Widow's Penny Rubbings, page 158
- ◎ Song: "If You're Happy and You Know It," page 172
- ◎ Snack: First Fruits Ices, page 199

LAZARUS (John 11:38-44)
- ◎ Games: Lazarus, Come Forth!, page 113
  Who Am I?, page 126
- ◎ Craft: Lazarus' Tombstone, page 148
- ◎ Song: "Father Abraham," page 169
- ◎ Snack: Sun Sippers, page 201

JESUS' MIRACLES (Luke 18:35-43)
- ◎ Game: Drawing Blind, page 107
- ◎ Craft: Ocean in a Bottle, page 149
- ◎ Song: "Jesus Loves Me," page 174
- ◎ Snack: Fishes and Loaves Snack Mix,
  page 200

EASTER (Luke 24:1-8)
- ◎ Game: Egg Roll, page 108
- ◎ Craft: Bunny's Big Heart, page 140
- ◎ Song: "Christ the Lord Is Risen Today,"
  page 167
- ◎ Snack: Wooden Cross Pretzels, page 211

THE BIBLE (2 Timothy 3:16)
- ◎ Game: Bible Charades, page 103
  New, Old or Not At All?, page 115
- ◎ Craft: Bible Scrolls, page 138
- ◎ Song: "The B-I-B-L-E," page 166
- ◎ Snack: Manna Burgers, page 202

PLAYTIME!

THE BEST PART ABOUT BABYSITTING is you get paid to play! Kids get bored playing with the same toys. Suggest one of these games when they are ready to do something different. Some have biblical tie-ins and some are just fun! Here are some easy ways to keep the kids (and you!) entertained.

BABIES

◎ COME AND GET ME

Hide behind a chair or sofa and say, "Evan, come and get me. Can you find me?" Once he looks around the chair and discovers where you are hiding, say, "You found me!" Or crawl around on the floor with the baby and say, "Are you following me?"

◎ CREEPY MOUSE

Use two fingers to walk up the baby's chest as you say, "Creep, creep, creep, creep…" Once your hand reaches under her neck, tickle her and say, "Creepy mouse!"

◎ FALLING TOWERS

Spread a blanket on the floor to sit on with the baby. Place with some safe, colorful toys within the baby's reach, such as blocks. Stack the blocks and let the baby knock them over. The baby will probably play this game as long as you keep stacking the blocks for him.

◎ FEEL THE WORLD

While holding the baby, stroll through the house in search of different textures to feel. Allow her to

touch textures like grainy sandpaper, fluffy pillows and slippery shower curtains. Describe aloud how each surface feels (soft, bumpy, scratchy).

◎ MiRROR, MiRROR On THE WALL

Place baby on the floor within reach of a floor length mirror. Sit on the floor beside the baby and ask, "Where is Lucy's nose?" Touch her nose in the reflection and say, "There is Lucy's nose!"

◎ PEEK-A-BOO

You are sure to get a smile with this one! Cover the baby's head with his blanket or a scarf. When you or the baby pulls off the blanket, say, "Peek-a-boo!"

TERRiFiC TiP!

BABY PATROL

If you are taking care of a baby, watch for small objects around the house that the baby could choke on, such as buttons, coins or paper clips. Babies put everything into their mouths!

~DANiELLE, 12
JACKSOn, mS

◎ SinG A SonG

Babies love to hear singing. They don't even seem to mind if you can't carry a tune! Try singing "Jesus Loves Me," "If You're Happy and You Know It," or "This Little Light of Mine." You'll find these and other great songs in *Music for the Heart* starting on page 163. Playing music while you "waltz" around the room with the baby in your arms is fun, too. One warning, though: avoid too much movement after baby has just eaten or your dance might end rather messily!

TODDLERS AND PRESCHOOLERS

◎ CITY BUS

Line up dining room or kitchen chairs in two rows with an aisle down the center. Let the child pretend to be the bus driver while you are the passenger, and vice versa.

◎ DRESS UP!

Kids love to pretend. Bring outgrown clothes or old costumes from home for the children to dress up in. Thrift shops are great places to find fake furs, feather wraps and scarves for dress up, and the prices are next to nothing!

◎ MAKE A ROCK BOX

A rock box is like a sandbox without the mess. Fill the bottom of a shoe box with fish tank gravel or small, smooth stones. Have small cups and beach tools on hand for filling and dumping. When the children are finished playing, replace the box top and store the box on a high shelf until it is time for you to go home.

◎ REPRINTS

With a crayon and paper, a child can make rubbings of coins, leaves or any other textured surfaces. Have the child place the paper over the object and rub it with the flat surface of a crayon.

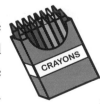

◎ TUB PAINT

Kids love to paint and create masterpieces. Place foam containers to paint in the kitchen sink. When the children are finished, wash the mess away!

◎ WHERE DID IT GO?

Hide a small toy inside your pocket and challenge the child to find it.

PAINT YOU CAN EAT

It's okay for the kids to lick their fingers when they use this paint!

WHAT YOU NEED

◎ 1 box instant vanilla pudding

◎ food coloring

WHAT TO DO

1. Make the pudding by following the package instructions.

2. Divide the pudding into a few bowls.

3. Add several drops of food coloring to each bowl for color. Try mixing colors like red and blue to make purple, yellow and blue for green, or red and yellow to get orange.

4. Allow the children to use the mix as finger paint.

◎ PLAY CLAY

Children love to squeeze, mush and smash things! Use interesting kitchen utensils like the cheese grater or potato masher to create "textures" with play clay (see recipe below). Let the child feel the bumps and grooves, then roll up the play clay again and start all over.

PLAY CLAY TO MAKE

WHAT YOU NEED

◎ 1 cup flour

◎ ½ cup salt

◎ 2 teaspoons cream of tartar

◎ 1 cup water

◎ 1 tablespoon vegetable oil

◎ food coloring

WHAT TO DO

1. Mix flour, salt and cream of tartar in a saucepan.

2. Add water, oil and two drops of food coloring.

3. Place on very low heat until mixture turns rubbery.

4. Remove from heat and knead. Store in an airtight container.

ALONG THE NILE BEACH PARTY

Ages 4-12

The Israelites probably built plenty of sand castles with their kids while wandering in the desert for 40 years. The object of the game is to create a "dream castle."

WHAT YOU NEED

◎ large plastic tub or box

◎ play sand

◎ beach shovel and bucket

WHAT TO DO

1. Pour the sand into the tub or box.

2. Hide shells or other surprises for the players to dig up.

3. Give each player a shovel and bucket of water. Let each player create her "dream castle."

4. After all the players have a chance to build a castle, tell them about the story of the wise and foolish builders in Matthew 7:24-27.

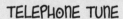

TERRIFIC TIP!

TELEPHONE TUNE

Impress the parents by helping little kids learn their telephone number. Sing the number to the tune of a song like "Mary Had a Little Lamb."

~MADDIE, 12
COLUMBIA, SC

BALLOON ORBIT

Ages 4-12

God placed all the moons, stars and planets in space. Now let's see if you can keep them in space! The object of the game is to keep the balloons in the air.

WHAT YOU NEED

◎ balloons

WHAT TO DO

1. Have all the players lay on the ground to form a circle.

2. Punch several balloons into the middle of the circle and have the players try to keep the "planets" (balloons) "orbiting" around.

3. Let the players pop any balloons that hit the ground.

• •

BIBLE CHARADES

Ages 6-12

Who is your favorite Bible hero? In this game you get to pretend to be one! The object of the game is to guess which Bible character and story each player is acting out.

WHAT YOU NEED

◎ paper

◎ pencil

WHAT TO DO

1. Try to use Bible stories that most children know well and can be acted out. Here is a list of some favorites:

◎ Noah's ark (Genesis 6:9-9:17)

◎ Moses and the Ten Commandments (Exodus 20:1-17)

◎ Joshua at the walls of Jericho (Joshua 5:13-6:27)

◎ Samson, the strongest man to live (Judges 13-16)

◎ Samuel hears God calling him (1 Samuel 3:1-21)

◎ Shadrach, Meshach and Abednego in the fiery furnace (Daniel 3)

◎ Daniel in the lions' den (Daniel 6:13-27)

◎ Jonah in the whale (Jonah 1-4)

◎ Jesus calms the sea (Matthew 8:23-27)

◎ Jesus walks on water (Mark 6:45-52)

◎ The empty tomb (Mark 16:1-8)

◎ Angel visits Mary, mother of Jesus (Luke 1:26-38)

◎ Jesus raises Lazarus from the dead (John 11:1-44)

2. Decide which stories are appropriate for the children's age levels. Divide the children into teams if there are more than three kids.

3. Write each Bible character with the Bible reference on separate slips of paper. Fold and place them in a hat for the players to draw out when it is their turn.

4. Gather any props or costumes you can find to add to the fun and excitement.

5. Take turns acting out each Bible character. The player that guesses correctly gets to act out the Bible charade on his paper.

BUBBLE MAGiC

All Ages

Everyone likes to play with bubbles! Pre-mix a batch at home, pour it into a container with a tight lid and put it in your Babysitter's Backpack. You'll be ready to "blow" at any time!

WHAT YOU NEED

◎ 2 cups water

◎ ¾ cup liquid dishwashing detergent

◎ ¼ cup corn syrup

◎ kitchen utensils

WHAT TO DO

1. Mix all of the ingredients together in a bowl. Store in a clean jar with a lid.

2. Pour ½ cup of liquid in a cup or bowl for each child. Use kitchen utensils to blow bubbles.

CLOUDS OF RAiN RELAY

Ages 4-12

It rained and rained and rained before Noah saw that first rainbow. Here's a fun way to make that point! The object of the game is to fill the dry land (bowl) with water first, using a wet sponge (cloud full of rain).

WHAT YOU NEED

◎ CD or tape player

- Christian music CD or tape

- bucket full of water

- 2 bowls

- 2 sponges

WHAT TO DO

1. Place a bucketful of water at the "start" line and an empty bowl at the "finish" line.

2. Start the CD or tape player. While a song is playing, each player must carry her "cloud full of rain" (wet sponge) to the other end and "water the land" (fill the bowl with water) before the song ends.

3. Try adjusting the length of the race for older kids.

CREATION SENSATION

Ages 4-12

This game will help children learn and memorize God's creation order. The object of the game is to place the days of creation postcards in order (based on Genesis 1:1-31).

WHAT YOU NEED

- postcards or pictures (see below)

WHAT TO DO

1. You will need one postcard or picture for each day of creation: darkness/light, clouds/sky, plants/trees, sun/moon/stars, animals/birds/fish, people.

2. Scramble the pictures on a table.

3. Read Genesis 1:1-31 to the children.

4. Ask the children to put the postcards in the correct order according to God's creation. (For instance, day one: darkness/light; day two: clouds/sky; day three: plants/trees and so on.)

5. After each child has taken a turn, tell the children the correct order, if they haven't already figured it out.

● ●

DRAWING BLIND

Ages 4-12

Imagine not being able to see! This game shows what it is like to be blind and how Jesus is able to heal. The object of the game is to draw a picture in the dark about the story of the blind beggar receiving his sight, as told by the babysitter.

WHAT YOU NEED

◎ pencil

◎ paper

WHAT TO DO

1. Give each player a sheet of paper and a pencil. When everyone is ready, turn the lights out to darken the room.

2. You act as the storyteller. Slowly describe the story in Luke 18:35-43. For example, you might say, "As Jesus approached Jericho…Please draw Jesus." All the players should do their best to draw a figure of Jesus. After a minute or so, continue with the story by adding, "A blind man was sitting by the roadside begging. Now draw the blind man sitting by the roadside." Other items the players can draw as you finish the story might be: the crowds of people, palm trees and the town.

3. At the end of the story, when the blind man receives his sight, turn on the lights for everyone to see their funny artwork.

● ●

EGG ROLL

Ages 4-8

Another version of this game has become a tradition on the White House lawn at Easter. The egg symbolizes the stone that was rolled away from Jesus' tomb when He was resurrected on Easter. The object of the game is to get your egg across the finish line first.

WHAT YOU NEED

◎ plastic or hard-boiled eggs

◎ spoons

WHAT TO DO

1. Give each player a spoon and an egg. All players line up at the start line.

2. Each player must roll an egg to the finish line, pushing it along with a spoon. The first one to cross the finish line is the winner.

3. Try adjusting the length of the race for older children.

TERRIFIC TIP!

A KEY POINT

When you go outside to play with the kids, take a house key with you just in case the door gets locked.

~HEATHER, 12
EAU CLAIRE, WI

GO FISH!

Ages 4-12

Everyone will be familiar with this game. But this time, you can remind the players that they are to be "fishers of men." The object of this game is to gather the most sets of two matching cards (for example: two hearts, two clubs, two spades and two diamonds) or be the first to get rid of all the cards in your hand. Note: Some families' religious beliefs do not allow for playing card games. Ask the parents before you bring cards to their home.

WHAT YOU NEED

◎ deck of cards

WHAT TO DO

1. Deal five cards face down to each player.

2. Place the remaining cards face down in the center.

3. Starting with the dealer, each player should call out another player's name and ask that player to hand over the cards he or she needs.

4. If the other player doesn't have any of the cards asked for, she says, "Go fish!"

5. The player who asked must pick a card from the center pile.

6. A player can repeat her turn over and over as long as she gets the card(s), she has requested from another player or the center pile.

7. If the player doesn't get the card she wants, she loses her turn and another player gets a turn.

HA-HA-HA HALLELUJAH

Ages 4-12

Laughter can be contagious. This game is sure to put a smile on everyone's faces. The object of this game is to keep a straight face while other players try to make you laugh.

WHAT TO DO

1. Have all the players sit in a circle.

2. The first player says "Ha." The next player says, "Ha-Ha." Then the next player says, "Ha-Ha-Ha" and so on.

3. Players must keep a straight face. If a player laughs, he or she is out of the game. The player who lasts the longest without laughing is the winner.

HEARTS!

Ages 8-12

Esther was truly the queen of hearts. In fact, playing cards originated in Old Testament times. The object of the game is to lose every hand that contains a heart. The player with the lowest number of penalty points wins the game.

WHAT YOU NEED

◎ deck of cards

◎ pencil

◎ paper

1. Shuffle the cards and deal 13 cards to each player. Pile the remaining cards face down in the middle of the table.

2. The first player takes a turn by placing a card face up next to the stack of cards.

3. The next player must play a card of the same suit as the first player. If he doesn't have a card of that suit, he can put down another card, but it will count as "less" than the other player's.

4. The player who plays the highest card of the suit (aces are highest) wins the hand. The winner of the hand gets to take a card from the stack (the loser takes the next card) and goes first in the next round. The game continues until all the cards in the pile are used and the cards in hand are played out.

5. To tally the scores: A player gets 1 penalty point for every heart won, 2 penalty points for the jack of hearts, 3 for the queen of hearts, 4 for the king of hearts and 5 for the ace. If a player happens to collect all 13 hearts, all of that player's penalty points are wiped out and his score is zero!

HiDE AND GO SHEEP

Ages 4-8

Kids love hide and seek. Now you can introduce them to one of Jesus' parables by using a game that is similar to that traditional game. The object of the game is to find the lost sheep.

WHAT YOU NEED

◎ cardboard

◎ scissors

◎ cotton balls

◎ tape

WHAT TO DO

1. Tell the parable of the lost sheep in Matthew 18:12-14 while the children cut a figure of a sheep out of cardboard.

2. For wool, they should tape cotton balls on the sheep's body.

3. After reading the story, have the children close their eyes while you hide the sheep. Announce to the children that one of the sheep is missing.

4. Encourage the children to look for the "lost sheep." When a child finds the sheep, have everyone shout and rejoice.

• •

THE INVISIBLE GIFT

Ages 4-12

Eternal life is an invisible gift from God. We can't touch it or see it, but it's real! This game will help the children learn about what is real. The object of this game is to identify the invisible gift (based on John 3:16).

WHAT TO DO

1. Have the players sit in a circle.

2. The first player should secretly think of a gift (can be an animal, toy, clothes, etc.) and pretend to hold it, then pass it on to the next player. For instance, if the player pretends the item is a dog, she can pretend to pet it, feed it, kiss it, hold it, etc. The player can only use hand motions. No talking is allowed.

3. The next player pretends to take the item and continues around the circle. The last player announces to the group what she thinks it is. If she is wrong, the next to last player takes a guess, and so on. If no one knows, the first player reveals to everyone what it was.

4. At the end of the game, tell the children about God's gift of eternal life, which is also invisible but much more important.

JONAH'S PAPER TAG

Ages 4-12

When God told Jonah to go to the city of Nineveh, Jonah got up and ran away instead. But Jonah couldn't outrun God. God made a big fish come along and swallow Jonah! Here's a fun tag game to remind you that you can't outrun God. The object of this game is to rip off the other player's belt before he gets yours.

WHAT YOU NEED

◎ crepe paper (two different colors)

WHAT TO DO

1. Play this tag game in a fenced yard. Divide the players into two teams.

2. Each player gets a 5-foot strip of crepe paper. They should tie the crepe paper around their waists like a belt, leaving a 3-foot tail. Each team should have its own color.

3. If a player gets his belt ripped off, he has to sit out the rest of the game.

4. To make the game last longer, designate a "safe" home base.

LAZARUS, COME FORTH!

Ages 4-12

When Jesus raised Lazarus from the dead, he was bound up like a mummy. Mary, Martha and friends had to unwrap him when he arose. In this game, you'll do just the opposite! The object of this game is to be the first player to wrap your partner "Lazarus" (based on John 11:1-44).

WHAT YOU NEED

◎ white toilet paper

◎ tape

WHAT TO DO

1. You will need one roll of toilet paper per team.

2. Divide the children into pairs (if there are enough). One player is Lazarus, the other is the wrapper.

3. The players should race to wrap their Lazarus from head to toe before the other team finishes. They can use tape if the paper tears.

4. After the game, read the story to the children of Jesus raising Lazarus from the dead.

LET THERE BE LIGHT

Ages 4-12

The Bible tells us not to hide our lights under bushels. Here's a game that demonstrates just that! The object of the game is to find the light hidden under the bushes.

WHAT YOU NEED

◎ several flashlights

WHAT TO DO

1. After it begins to get dark outside, have the children close their eyes while you hide lit flashlights around the yard or house.

2. Make sure every child gets a chance to find a flashlight.

3. Tell the children how God created light in the book of Genesis. You could also tell them the parable of the light hidden under a bowl in Matthew 5:15-16.

• •

NEW, OLD OR NOT AT ALL?

Ages 6-12

This game will introduce children to the Bible and test their knowledge. The object of this game is to identify whether the person, place or thing is from the New Testament, Old Testament or if it is not in the Bible.

WHAT YOU NEED

◎ 3" x 5" cards

◎ black marker

WHAT TO DO

1. Write on different 3" x 5" cards the words "New," "Old" and "Not at All" for each player.

2. Tell the children you will call out a name (for example: Moses) from the Bible or someplace else.

3. Have each player give his answer by holding up the correct card. Add to the excitement by having everyone answer at the same time.

4. Try calling out fun names such as celebrities, names of places, presidents, etc.

DRINK UP

If you are playing with the kids outside on a hot day, make sure everyone drinks a lot of water so they don't get dehydrated.

~CARRIE, 11
LARAMIE, WY

PHARAOH'S FROGS

Ages 6-12

This game will get the kids hopping! What better way to learn about the Jews' exodus from Egypt? The object of the game is to get through the plagues of Egypt (based on Exodus 7-11).

WHAT YOU NEED

◎ red liquid (juice, punch or colored water)

◎ marshmallows

◎ bandanna or scarf

WHAT TO DO

1. Have one player go to the end of the yard. Blindfold (plague of darkness) him.

2. Have another player stand near the house with a cup of red liquid (plague of blood) and marshmallows (plague of hail) beside him.

3. On "go," the blindfolded player must leap like a frog (plague of frogs) toward the other player, who may only "moo" (plague of livestock) like a cow to give directions. They may work out a special signal code in advance. For instance, one "moo" could mean "turn left," two "moos" could mean "turn right."

4. Once the blindfolded player reaches the "moo" player, he must find the marshmallows and red drink and feed them to him. Then the blindfolded player leaps back to where they began. If there are more than two players, have other blindfolded "frog" and "moo" players.

5. After the game, tell the children about the plagues of Egypt and what each one represented.

PIN THE STONE ON GOLIATH

Ages 4-12

David wasn't afraid to stand up to the giant. Neither are we! The object of the game is to pin the stone on Goliath's head. The player who gets the closest wins.

WHAT YOU NEED

◎ poster board

◎ markers

◎ balloons

◎ tape

◎ blindfold (bandanna)

WHAT TO DO

1. Introduce the game by reading or telling the story of David and Goliath. You can find the story in 1 Samuel 17:1-58. It's a long chapter, so you may want to use a children's story book or devotional.

2. On poster board, draw a picture of a large giant with an extra-large head. Use small or partially-filled balloons as stones.

3. Put a rolled piece of tape on each balloon.

4. Take turns blindfolding each child and let him or her try to place the "stone" on Goliath after a few spins.

Remember your Creator in the days of your youth.

~ Ecclesiastes 12:1

PRAYER TAG

Ages 4-12

Here's a fun game to remind everyone to pray. The object of the game is to not get tagged by It.

WHAT TO DO

1. Prayer Tag is like the traditional game of tag with one person as It. Players in Prayer Tag are safe from It if they drop to their knees and clasp their hands in an attitude of prayer when It approaches.

2. It must take five giant steps back, during which time the player on his or her knees must get up and run or risk being tagged.

3. Once a player is tagged, he or she becomes It.

RED LIGHT, GREEN LIGHT

Ages 4-8

This is an oldie but goodie! The object of the game is to be the first one to tag the police officer without getting caught.

WHAT YOU NEED

◎ two ropes

WHAT TO DO

1. Play this tag game in a fenced yard. Lay down two ropes to mark the starting line and finish line.

2. Designate one player to be the police officer and have her stand in front of one line. All the other players should stand behind the opposite line.

3. The game begins when the police officer turns her back and yells, "Green light!" then counts loudly to 5. The other players must run as fast as they can toward the police officer while she counts. When the police officer finishes counting, she should yell, "Red light!" The players must freeze instantly.

4. The police officer turns around quickly to catch any players still moving. Anyone who is caught moving must return to the start line.

5. The game continues until one of the players crosses over the finish line while the police officer's back is still turned. That player then becomes the police officer.

SEEK AND FIND

Ages 6-12

Here's a fun way to learn scriptures. The object of this game is to solve all the hidden clues. Each clue leads the player to the next clue. At the last clue, a prize waits for the winner.

WHAT YOU NEED

◎ 3" x 5" index cards

◎ black pen or marker

◎ tape

◎ small prizes (candy or special treat)

WHAT TO DO

1. Write on each index card a Scripture containing your clue. Listed below are some suggestions. Try adding some of your own!

2. While the children hide their eyes, tape all of the clue cards at each designated place. Remember, the clue for the bedroom door, for example, is not placed on the bedroom door. The next clue, the clue for the living room lamp, is taped to the bedroom door. Try to keep the cards in order to avoid confusion.

3. Explain that they must look for keywords in each Scripture to know where to go next. You may need to help them with the first one to get them started.

4. Have a special treat waiting for them at the end.

SUGGESTED SCRIPTURES FOR CLUES

◎ *But when you pray, go into your room, close the door and pray to your Father, who is unseen.* Matthew 6:6 (Answer: children's bedroom door)

◎ *When Jesus spoke again to the people, he said, "I am the light of the world. Whoever follows me will never walk in darkness, but will have the light of life."* John 8:12 (Answer: living room lamp)

◎ *Look at the birds of the air; they do not sow or reap or store away in barns, and yet your heavenly Father feeds them. Are you not much more valuable than they?* Matthew 6:26 (Answer: birdhouse or bird feeder)

◎ *He cuts off every branch in me that bears no fruit, while every branch that does bear fruit he prunes so that it will be even more fruitful.* John 15:2 (Answer: tree outside)

◎ *Anyone who touches his bed must wash his clothes and bathe with water, and he will be unclean till evening.* Leviticus 15:5 (Answer: washing machine)

◎ *They set the tables, they spread the rugs, they eat, they drink!* Isaiah 21:5 (Answer: kitchen table)

◎ *All night long on my bed I looked for the one my heart loves.* Song of Songs 3:1 (Answer: bed)

◎ *Your teeth are like a flock of sheep just shorn, coming up from the washing.* Song of Songs 4:2 (Answer: bathroom, toothbrush)

◎ *I have drunk...my milk.* Song of Songs 5:1 (Answer: milk in the refrigerator)

◎ *Do not work for food that spoils, but for food that endures to eternal life, which the Son of Man will give you.* John 6:27 (Answer: kitchen pantry)

◎ *When they landed, they saw a fire of burning coals there with fish on it, and some bread.* John 21:9 (Answer: barbecue grill or fireplace)

◎ *So she let them down by a rope through the window, for the house she lived in was part of the city wall.* Joshua 2:15 (Answer: window)

• •

SIDEWALK GRAPEFRUIT BOWL

Ages 4-12

This game is simply for fun! Like bowling, the object of the game is to knock over all the pins.

WHAT YOU NEED

◎ grapefruit or orange

◎ empty, clean 2-liter soda bottles

WHAT TO DO

1. Set up the empty soda bottles at one end of the sidewalk as bowling pins.

2. Have the children roll the grapefruit like a bowling ball and see who can knock down the most pins.

• •

SNAP, CRACKLE POPPING BUBBLES

Ages 4-8

Everyone loves to play with bubbles. They seem to dazzle all kids. The object of the game is to have fun blowing bubbles and hearing them pop.

WHAT YOU NEED

◎ Bubble Magic (see page 105)

◎ spatula

◎ strainer

◎ cookie cutters

WHAT TO DO

1. On a cold, crisp winter day, take the children outside to experience bubble-blowing a whole new way — the bubbles freeze!

2. Stand near the porch light so you can watch the bubbles glisten. Listen carefully as the bubbles hit the ground. Ask the children to describe what they hear.

● ●

STRONG AS SAMSON

All Ages

The object of this game is to pump up "Samson's" muscles by stuffing the most balloons into his suit (based on Judges 16:1-31).

WHAT YOU NEED

◎ 25-30 small, partially-inflated balloons

◎ 2 extra large pants and long-sleeved shirts

WHAT TO DO

1. Divide the children into two teams (if there are enough). Select one player to be Samson. The other players will be his personal trainers.

2. Divide the balloons equally between the two teams. Each Samson puts on the extra large clothing over his own clothing.

3. Each team should try to pump up Samson's muscles by stuffing balloons inside his extra large clothing.

4. Give each team 2 minutes to stuff balloons. When the time is up, count how many balloons are left over. The team with the fewest balloons wins!

5. Read the Bible story about Samson to the kids.

UP YOUR SLEEVE

Ages 4-8

You can use your imagination on this game. You may want to add Christian items that you can use as props to share your faith. The object of the game is to identify each item by "feel" and "touch."

WHAT YOU NEED

◎ 1 large coffee can or baby formula can

◎ 1 athletic sock

◎ various small objects (buttons, toys, combs, etc.)

WHAT TO DO

1. Place the objects inside the coffee can.

2. Cut off the top of the sock and slip it over the can.

3. Call out the name of an item, then have a child try to find the object by feeling for it.

WATER-BALLOON TOSS

Ages 4-12

Everyone will love this game, just be set to get wet! The object of the game is to toss as many water balloons as possible without them bursting.

WHAT YOU NEED

◎ water balloons

WHAT TO DO

1. Here's a way to cool off the kids outside on a hot day. Make several water balloons before starting the game.

2. Gather all the players into a circle. Toss a water balloon to a player in the circle and have the players begin to toss it around the circle. Continue to add water balloons to the circle until all the players are juggling as many as possible.

3. Remind the players to keep the balloons moving. Have fun getting everyone wet!

TERRIFIC TIP!

SIMPLE INTEREST

Little kids can't pay attention to one thing for a long time, so it's a good idea to change activities at least once an hour.

~HANNAH, 13
DES MOINES, IA

WATER-GUN VOLLEYBALL

Ages 6-12

Older kids will love this! The object of the game is for one team to score the most points.

WHAT YOU NEED

◎ 1 squirt gun per child

◎ 2-3 balloons

◎ tape or string

WHAT TO DO

1. Outline a rectangular area in the yard. Divide the playing area in half with tape or string on the ground. Form two teams and have the players sit down on either side of the line.

2. Inflate two to three balloons. Give each child a loaded squirt gun.

3. Play volleyball using the balloon as a ball. Tell the players they must squirt their guns as many times as necessary to move the balloon over the line.

4. If the balloon touches the ground on the team A side, team B gets a point and vice-versa.

WETBALL

Ages 6-12

You've heard the song "Take Me Out to the Ball Game." Well, maybe this isn't quite the same, but it's the next best thing to being there! The object of the game is for one team to score the most points.

WHAT YOU NEED

◉ tennis racket

◉ 2 sponge-type balls

◉ bucket full of water

WHAT TO DO

1. When the weather is sizzling hot outside, have the children put on their bathing suits for this wet game.

2. Set up three "bases" and a "home plate" as in baseball. The tennis racket and sponge balls will be used in place of a bat and baseball.

3. Place the water bucket next to the pitcher, so that the sponge ball can be soaked before pitching. Have one sponge ball soaking while the other is pitched.

4. Each batter has three tries to hit the wet sponge ball. An "out" occurs when the batter fails to hit the ball or when a runner is hit by the wet sponge ball while running between bases.

5. Play as many innings as you like!

WHO AM I?

Ages 6-12

Here's a great way to introduce children to favorite Bible characters. Like the traditional game of 20 Questions, the object of this game is to guess the Bible Hero within 20 yes or no questions.

WHAT YOU NEED

◉ 3" x 5" cards

◉ black marker

WHAT TO DO

1. Write Bible hero names on the cards. For example: Noah, David, Solomon and so on.

2. One player chooses a card and secretly looks at it.

3. The other players must ask yes and no questions, to figure out who the Bible Hero is.

4. If a player incorrectly guesses who the Bible Hero is, he or she is out of the game. If no one has guessed correctly after 20 questions have been asked, the player reads the card aloud for everyone and wins! If a player correctly guesses within the 20 questions, then he or she draws a card, and gets a chance to stump everyone.

THE WIDOW'S PENNY

Ages 6-12

This game will remind the children that the widow gave all she had to Jesus. The object of the game is to win the most pennies.

WHAT YOU NEED

◎ 20-25 pennies (need 5 pennies per child)

WHAT TO DO

1. Spread five pennies on the floor in front of a wall. Give each player five pennies.

2. Tell the first player to gently toss a penny against the wall, aiming so that the penny will ricochet and hit one of the pennies on the floor.

3. If a player hits one of the pennies on the floor, he or she gets to pick up the penny that was thrown and the one it hit. If the penny hits more than one, he or she gets to keep all the pennies hit.

4. If the penny thrown doesn't hit any other pennies, it stays on the ground where it lands and the next player takes his or her turn.

5. Tell the children about the widow in Luke 21:1-4.

He will yet fill your mouth with laughter and your lips with shouts of joy.

~ Job 8:21

LiGHTS, POPCORN, ViDEO!

YOU'RE SET. You've turned down the lights. Popped the popcorn (see page 134). Slid the video into the VCR. Now you're ready to sit back and relax for the next couple of hours while the kids are plopped in front of the TV. But is the movie or TV show you are about to watch appropriate for children?

CHOOSING THE RIGHT VIDEO

A good rule of thumb when choosing a video to watch is:

Does the movie violate any of the Ten Commandments? (Exodus 20:1-17)

If so, it is not appropriate for viewing. God wants you to share His truth. The Bible tells us to guard our hearts, souls and minds. Choose a movie that will reflect Bible truths. It doesn't necessarily have to be a "Christian" video, but one that will uphold the values of a true believer in Christ. To know if your video honors God, apply this checklist to it:

Does the movie exalt any other gods? Does it contain witchcraft, sorcery or demons? Choose a movie that shows the power of the living God.

You shall have no other gods before me.

~ Exodus 20:3

Does the movie promote idol worship? Does the movie promote other religions, such as bowing before a statue of Buddha? Choose a movie that reflects the truth.

You shall not make for yourself an idol in the form of anything in heaven above or on the earth beneath or in the waters below. You shall not bow down to them or worship them; for I, the Lord your God, am a jealous God.

~ Exodus 20:4-5

Does the movie contain profanity or use the name of God or Jesus in vain? Just about any movie rated PG, PG-13 or R contains swearing. Only G-rated movies are profanity-free.

You shall not misuse the name of the Lord your God, for the Lord will not hold anyone guiltless who misuses his name.

~ Exodus 20:7

Does the movie respect and honor God? Choose a movie that will encourage godly behavior.

Remember the Sabbath day by keeping it holy.

~ Exodus 20:8

Does the movie encourage children to obey their parents? Many movies today show kids rebelling against their parents. Choose a movie that encourages family values.

Honor your father and your mother, so that you may live long in the land the Lord your God is giving you.

~ Exodus 20:12

Does the movie contain murders or violence? Choose a movie that encourages helping others.

You shall not murder.

~Exodus 20:13

Does the movie contain sex? Choose a movie that encourages keeping the marriage vow or the purity vow.

You shall not commit adultery.

~Exodus 20:14

Does the movie glorify stealing or theft? Choose a movie that encourages honesty.

You shall not steal.

~ Exodus 20:15

 Is the movie based on a lie? Choose a movie that encourages truthfulness.

You shall not give false testimony against your neighbor.

~ Exodus 20:16

 Is the movie about lust or greed? Choose a movie that encourages contentment.

You shall not covet your neighbor's house. You shall not covet your neighbor's wife, or his manservant or maidservant, his ox or donkey, or anything that belongs to your neighbor.

~ Exodus 20:17

If the movie you selected gets a "thumbs down" for any of these commandments, you should select another video to watch.

A WORD on THE WAY

Whatever is true, whatever is noble, whatever is right, whatever is pure, whatever is lovely, whatever is admirable — if anything is excellent or praiseworthy — think about such things.

~ Philippians 4:8

A SAFE BET

The checklist is a good reminder that most movies and TV shows do not honor God. But that doesn't mean you cannot watch a video or TV. You can find a variety of family-valued, Bible-based videos for rent or purchase at most Christian bookstores. With so many to choose from, it should be easy to find one that matches your theme. You can also rest  assured that it will be safe to watch with no non-Christian surprises. If Christian videos are not available, play it safe and only show videos rated "G". The kids may protest that their parents allow them to watch other types of videos and TV shows, and they may, but use your babysitting time to encourage good values.

POPCORN iS FUN TO MAKE AND EAT!

Stash a bag of popcorn in your Babysitter's Backpack for when you plan to watch a video. Follow the package instructions to prepare it. Stay with the bag as it cooks. Some microwaves will cook popcorn in 3 minutes, while others may take 5 or 6 minutes. But be safe rather than sorry so you don't get a bag of scorched, smelly popcorn!

After you remove the bag, carefully open it at the top by slowly pulling the diagonal corners. Be sure to guard yourself from the steam that will escape from the bag as you open it. Do not allow the children to open the bag because the hot steam could cause severe burns. Also, do not serve popcorn to kids 3 and under because they could choke on it.

134

COOL KID CRAFTS!

THE CRAFTS IN THIS SECTION were developed to go with the *Babysitter Bible Themes*. They can be easily made using inexpensive materials, and can usually be completed during one babysitting session. Feel free to develop your own!

These projects were selected to not only entertain the children, but to introduce them to the Bible and who God is. When a child completes a craft, he or she will gain a sense of accomplishment. Over time, the child will hopefully develop an interest in knowing God more personally.

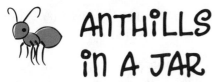

ANTHILLS IN A JAR

Ages 4-12

Who doesn't love ants? Maybe we would rather they not invade at a picnic, but they are fun to watch behind glass.

WHAT YOU NEED

◎ large glass jars with lids (mayonnaise or peanut butter jar)

◎ small glass jars with lids (jelly or baby food jars)

◎ sandy soil

◎ birdseed or grass seed

◎ ½ teaspoon water with sugar added

WHAT TO DO

1. You will need one large glass jar with a lid and two small glass jars, one with a lid, per child.

2. Show how to place the small jar turned upside down with no lid inside the large jar.

3. Help the kids pour the soil into the large jar, around and over the top of the jar inside until it is covered.

4. Give the kids the small jar with a lid to go outside and find ants for their ant villages. Help them look along sidewalks or under stones. Show how to lay a piece of paper down for the ants to crawl on, like a ramp. Assist the kids as a they gently slide the ants into the small jar. Have them cover the jar with the lid to keep the ants from getting out.

4. Help the kids carefully pour the ants into the large jar. Allow them to drop a few seeds and water inside the jar.

5. Tightly screw on the top of the large jar. Keep the jar out of direct sunlight. Have fun watching the ants tunnel their way through the village!

• •

 # BiBLE SCROLLS

All Ages

In Revelation, God instructed John to eat the "little book." The Bible is our spiritual food because it feeds our souls. Make these scrolls as a reminder to read your Bible!

WHAT YOU NEED
• • • • • • • • • • • •

◎ refrigerated crescent roll dough

◎ honey

◎ baking sheet

◎ non-stick cooking spray

◎ paper plates

WHAT TO DO

1. Preheat the oven at the temperature suggested on the crescent roll package.

2. Give each child a paper plate and place two triangle sections of the dough (still connected) on it.

3. Flatten the dough and have the child dip a spoonful of honey out and drizzle the words, "God's Law," on the dough.

4. Have the child roll the rectangle from both ends to make a scroll, then place the scrolls on the cookie sheet. Bake 8-10 minutes.

5. While the scrolls are baking, talk to the children about how important it is to read the Bible and do what it says.

 # BOX CHARIOT

Ages 4-8

Elijah rode up to heaven in a chariot of fire! Here's a chariot to make.

WHAT YOU NEED

◎ medium-size boxes

◎ aluminum foil

◎ construction paper

◎ paper fasteners

◎ scissors

◎ tape

WHAT TO DO
• • • • • • • • • • •

1. Help the kids cut out the bottom and top of a box, leaving the four sides as the body of the chariot.

2. Show how to cover the sides with aluminum foil, taping it underneath.

3. Help the kids cut two circles from the extra cardboard to create wheels for the chariot. Punch a hole in the middle of each circle. Show how to attach one circle to each side of the chariot with a paper fastener.

4. Have the children design their own emblem from construction paper and tape it to the front of the chariot.

5. Tell the story of Elijah, who was taken to heaven in a chariot, in 2 Kings 2:1-18. Then have a chariot race!

• •

BUNNY'S BIG HEART

Ages 6-12

This craft can be made as a Valentine or for Easter. Inside the bunny's body is a big surprise!

WHAT YOU NEED
• • • • • • • • • • • • • •

◎ pink paper

◎ scissors

◎ black marker

◎ stapler

◎ tape

◎ glue

◎ flat lollipop

WHAT TO DO

1. Show how to fold a piece of pink paper in half and cut a half heart along the fold. Leave the heart folded to form the body of the bunny.

2. Have the kids cut a smaller heart from pink paper for the bunny's head. They can use a black marker to draw eyes, nose and a mouth on the bunny.

3. Staple the head to the pointed end of the heart body. Staple the heart body at the rounded top to form a pocket. Cover the staples with tape so the kids don't injure themselves on the prongs.

4. Instruct the kids to cut a small heart from the pink paper and write "pull" on it. They should glue the heart to the stick end of a lollipop.

5. Show how to tuck the lollipop into the body of the bunny so that the stick end with the small heart is poking out to form the tail.

 DAViD'S SLiNGSHOT WHEEL

Ages 4-12

David's slingshot went round and round like this pinwheel. This traditional toy is sure to be a kid-pleaser!

WHAT YOU NEED

- colored construction paper
- straight pin
- tape
- new pencil
- crayons
- scissors

WHAT TO DO

1. Cut a large square out of the colored construction paper, making sure all sides are equal. Have the children draw a slingshot on one corner and a stone on every other corner, so when the wheel it spins it will look like the stone is being thrown.

2. Have the kids draw an X on the paper from corner to corner.

3. Instruct the kids to cut along these diagonal lines up to about where the dot is shown on the diagram. Do not cut all the way to the center!

4. Show how to bend corner 1 toward the center as shown. Bend corner 2 toward the center, overlapping corner 1, as shown. Repeat this for all four corners. Tape to secure.

5. Poke a straight pin through the center of the slingshot wheel and into the pencil's eraser. Make sure the wheel can spin freely.

6. Show how to hold the slingshot wheel up to catch a breeze and whirl around!

142

FiRE on THE mounTAin

Ages 4-12

Everyone will love this craft! Use it as a lesson about how God spoke to Moses through a burning bush. It's based on Exodus 3:1-21.

WHAT YOU NEED

◎ baking sheet

◎ small bowl

◎ red food coloring

◎ vinegar

◎ baking soda

WHAT TO DO

1. Place two tablespoons of baking soda in a bowl. Set the bowl on the cookie sheet.

2. Add several drops of red food coloring to the vinegar. Replace cap and shake.

3. Pour the vinegar over the baking soda and watch it foam!

O Lord, you are our Father. We are the clay, you are the potter; we are all the work of your hand.

~ Isaiah 64:8

GOD MADE ME

Ages 4-8

Now the kids can create like the Creator. Let the kids use their imaginations and be as creative as they like! This craft is based on Genesis 1:26-37.

WHAT YOU NEED

◎ play clay

◎ small beads, buttons, tacks, etc.

WHAT TO DO

1. Give each child a different color of play clay, if possible.

2. Tell everyone to create a creature or person, like God created animals and people in the Garden of Eden.

3. Show how to add decorative items for body parts, such as tacks for eyes.

4. Read the Scripture above aloud and tell the children that God made the first people from clay, too.

HOMEMADE STICKERS

Ages 4-12

Most kids love stickers, so this one is sure to be a hit!

WHAT YOU NEED

◎ 2 tablespoon white glue

◎ 1 tablespoon white vinegar

◎ vanilla or peppermint flavoring

◎ pictures or gift wrap

◎ scissors

◎ bowl

◎ measuring spoons

◎ paintbrush

WHAT TO DO

1. Mix the glue and vinegar together in a bowl until it is well-blended. Stir in two or three drops of flavoring.

2. Have the kids cut pictures or gift wrap into various shapes.

3. Show how to use the paintbrush to coat the back of the paper shapes with the glue and vinegar mixture.

4. Allow the solution to dry.

5. Tell the kids that when they are ready to use their stickers, they should just remoisten the back and stick!

i Am THUMBODY

Ages 4-12

Everybody is important to God and everyone is unique, just like your finger print! Here's a fun way to make thumbody important! It's based on Song of Songs 6:9.

WHAT YOU NEED

◎ paper

◎ finger paint or ink pad

◎ black marker

WHAT TO DO

1. Tell the children that God made each person unique. Explain how each one of us has our own unique thumb print.

2. Have each child press his thumb into the ink pad or paint, then press it on the paper.

3. While the children draw legs, arms and a face on their thumbprints, read the Scripture above to them.

PAINT SOLUTION

If you are using paint in a craft and you start to run out of it, stretch it by mixing it with white glue and food coloring.

~MAGGiE, 12
OKLAHOMA CITY, OK

JONAH AND THE WHALE TOY

Ages 4-12

Poor Jonah! Can you imagine being stuck in the tummy of a whale for three days and nights with seaweed wrapped around your neck? That's what happened to Jonah. This craft allows kids to be the whale and swallow up Jonah.

WHAT YOU NEED

◎ markers

◎ scissors

◎ plastic liter bottle, empty

◎ plastic grocery bag

WHAT TO DO

1. Have the kids decorate a plastic bottle with markers to make a whale. The opening of the bottle should be the whale's mouth.

2. Show how to draw Jonah on a 3" x 3" piece of grocery bag and carefully cut him out.

3. Fill a sink or tub with water. Float Jonah in the water, then squeeze the whale and push him under the water. Swim Jonah over to the whale and slowly let out the sides of the bottle. The whale will swallow Jonah! Squeeze the bottle again to spit out Jonah.

LAZARUS' TOMBSTONE

Ages 4-12

In Bible times, the dead were buried in tombs or caves. Then large stones were placed in front of the opening. This craft can serve as a daily reminder of how Jesus raised Lazarus from the grave.

WHAT YOU NEED

◎ 3 or 4 crayons

◎ small bag

◎ rock

WHAT TO DO

1. Peel the wrappers off three or four old crayons. Place the crayons in a bag and have the kids help you smash them into little pieces using a rock.

2. Lay the rock on newspaper in the hot sun. Let the kids sprinkle the rock with crayon bits.

3. Leave the rock in the sun until the crayons melt over it, coating it with a colorful wax.

4. Bring the rock inside to cool. The wax will harden.

5. Let the kids give the rock to Mom or Dad to use as a paperweight.

OCEAN in A BOTTLE

Ages 6-12

This craft, which is based on Matthew 8:23, can be used with either the Jonah and the Whale theme or the Jesus' Miracles theme. Kids can create their own "storms" while you tell the story you choose.

WHAT YOU NEED

◎ 12-ounce jar with lid

◎ 6 ounces cooking oil

◎ 6 ounces white vinegar

◎ blue food coloring

◎ glue

WHAT TO DO

1. Pour the cooking oil into the clean jar, followed by the vinegar. Let the children watch as the liquids separate.

2. Add several drops of the food coloring into the jar. If available, place a small boat inside the jar.

3. Place glue around the lid and screw it on tightly.

4. Let the children shake the jar to make waves. Remind them that just like the ocean, this is a liquid you can't drink. (The liquid is non-toxic, but it wouldn't taste very good!)

5. While the children play with the ocean in the bottle, tell the story of Jonah and how the terrible storm came upon him when he ran from God. (Alternate story: Jesus calms the storm.)

QUEEN OF HEARTS

Ages 6-12

Esther was a special queen chosen by God to serve His people. Her example reminds us that no matter who we are, God can use us in powerful ways when we allow Him.

WHAT YOU NEED

◎ heart playing cards

◎ red chenille wire

◎ scissors

◎ red construction paper

◎ round lollipops

◎ black marker

◎ stapler

WHAT TO DO

1. You will need two heart playing cards for each child. Use one heart playing card for the front and the other card for the back.

2. For the arms and legs, help the kids cut a red chenille wire into

four pieces that are approximately 2" long. Staple the arms and legs between the two playing cards.

3. For the head, have the kids cut a heart shape from red construction paper and draw a face and crown using a black marker. Show how to staple the head to the top of the queen's body.

4. Show how to bend the bottom of the pipe cleaner legs to form feet.

5. Allow each kids to wrap one of the queen's arms around a lollipop (candy facing downward) which will prop her up.

● ●

 # RAIN CLOUDS

Ages 4-8

This craft will remind children that God made the clouds and rain. They can shake their clouds and create a storm.

WHAT TO DO
● ● ● ● ● ● ● ● ● ● ● ● ●

◎ aluminum foil or Christmas tree garland

◎ tape or glue

◎ cotton balls

◎ paper plates

◎ string or yarn

WHAT TO DO

1. Cut aluminum foil into ½" x 6" strips.

2. Have the kids tape or glue "raindrop" foil strips to a paper plate.

3. Show how to glue cotton balls to the paper plate to cover the tops of the foil and create fluffy clouds.

4. Punch holes on each side of the plate. Help the kids string a length of yarn through the holes. Knot each end and let the kids shake the plates to create a "rainstorm."

 # RAINBOW MUSH

Ages 4-12

Here's a fun way to remember God's promise to never flood the entire earth again.

WHAT YOU NEED

◎ 4 cups cold water

◎ 1 cup cornstarch

◎ ⅓ cup sugar

◎ food coloring (several colors)

◎ glitter (optional)

◎ resealable plastic sandwich bags

◎ spoon

◎ saucepan

◎ small bowls

◎ measuring cups

WHAT TO DO

1. In a saucepan, mix the cornstarch, sugar and water together until well blended.

2. Cook over medium heat, stirring constantly, until the mixture thickens (5-10 minutes).

3. Divide the gooey mixture into several bowls. Let the children stir a few drops of food coloring into each bowl. Try mixing some fun colors, such as red and blue for purple, yellow and blue for green or red and yellow for orange.

4. Once the mixture cools, spoon some of each color into plastic bags (one per child) and seal them tightly. If you want, you can add glitter to some of the gooey mixture to give it a little sparkle.

5. Allow the kids to squeeze and squish their rainbows for fun!

SAMSON'S HAIR FLIP BOOK

Ages 6-12

Samson was a "Nazirite" dedicated to God with a special vow: he was to never cut his hair. Unfortunately, his enemy tricked him, cut off his hair and threw him into prison. But God helped Samson regain his great strength by making his hair grow back. Now, you can watch Samson's hair grow with this flipbook. This craft will remind children that our strength comes from God.

WHAT YOU NEED

◎ patterns on pages 159 and 161

◎ small pad of paper or sticky notes

◎ pencil

◎ markers or crayons

◎ quarter

◎ push pin

CUT IT OUT

If there are little kids around, make sure scissors, knives and other sharp tools you are using for crafts are kept out of their reach.

~SOPHIE, 12
OMAHA, NE

WHAT TO DO

1. Stick a push pin through the center of the pad of paper.

2. Instruct the kids to trace around the quarter to draw Samson's head. They should use the pin mark as a guide to keep the illustrations in a consistent place on each page.

3. Have the kids add eyes, nose and a mouth to each page. They should draw the hair a little longer on each page. When the pages are quickly flipped through, it will look like Samson's hair is growing!

4. For a shortcut, make copies of pages 159 and 161 for the kids to color. Then cut out the drawings and paste them on a pad. This flip book has 24 pages. For smoother action, repeat each drawing twice (48 pages).

SAMUEL'S NIGHT LIGHT

Ages 6-12

Samuel was awakened at night by God. When he finally realized it was God, he answered and said, "I'm listening." This craft will remind the children to always listen to God and do what He says.

WHAT YOU NEED

◎ clay (on page 156)

◎ cooking oil

◎ linen cloth or wick

WHAT TO DO

1. Make the clay as directed on the next page.

2. Use the illustration as a guide to show how to shape the clay in the form of a Bible-times oil lamp.

3. Bake the clay at 225 degrees for two hours. Allow to cool.

4. Help the students fill the lamp with oil and float a piece of candle wick or linen cloth in the oil.

5. Tell the children to leave their oil lamps on the kitchen or dining room table so their parents can light them at dinnertime

CLAY

WHAT YOU NEED

◎ 1 cup salt

◎ ¾ cup water

◎ ½ cup cornstarch

WHAT TO DO

1. Mix salt, water and cornstarch in a saucepan.

2. Cook on low heat until the mixture thickens.

3. Cool on waxed paper. Knead for 3 minutes. Clay should be used right away.

4. Bake shaped clay at 225 degrees for 2 hours.

TWISTED SHEPHERD STAFFS

Ages 4-12

Here is an easy craft to make at Christmas time!

WHAT YOU NEED

◎ red chenille wire

◎ white chenille wire

WHAT TO DO

1. Show how to hold the red and white chenille wire together and twist to create candy stripes.

2. Show how to pull the tip of the wires down to form a hook or "J" shape.

3. While the children make their twisted shepherd staffs, share how the shepherds were in the fields watching their sheep at night when angels filled the sky, announcing Jesus' birth.

 # WALLS YOU CAN EAT

Ages 4-12

This craft is based on Hebrews 11:30. Kids will love building walls out of Oreo cookies, if they don't eat them all first! Make sure you have plenty of milk on hand.

WHAT YOU NEED

◎ package of Oreo cookies

◎ milk

◎ toothpicks

WHAT TO DO

1. Read the story about the walls of Jericho in Joshua 5:13-6:20 before starting the craft.

2. Ask the children to try to build a wall using Oreo cookies.

Show how to use the white cream in the centers of the cookies as "glue" or mortar. Connect the walls with toothpicks.

• •

WIDOW'S PENNY RUBBINGS

Ages 4-12

A penny is not worth much now, but giving everything you have to God is worth a lot to Him! Make these rubbings as a reminder to give to God.

WHAT YOU NEED

◎ white paper

◎ crayons or markers

◎ pencil

◎ pennies

WHAT TO DO

1. Give each child a sheet of paper. Across the top of the paper, have the child print, "Give All to Jesus."

2. Give each child a sharpened pencil and a couple of pennies.

3. Show how to make a "rubbing" of the front and back of a penny.

4. Allow the kids to add flair to their rubbings by coloring the rest of the page.

MUSIC FOR THE HEART

MUSIC SEEMS TO BRIGHTEN everyone's spirits. Children especially love to sing! The songs included in this chapter are for ages preschool through preteen and have been chosen to go along with the Bible story themes in this book. Most of the songs are well-known children's favorites or are sung to a familiar tune such as "London Bridge Is Falling Down" or "Ring Around the Rosy." If you are unfamiliar with a tune, make up your own and add action movements for fun, such as marching or clapping! Feel free to add your own favorite songs and lead a sing-along!

ARKY, ARKY

Traditional

FIRST VERSE

The Lord told Noah, "There's gonna be a floody, floody."
Lord told Noah, "There's gonna be a floody, floody."
Get those animals out of the muddy, muddy,
Children of the Lord.

CHORUS

So, rise and shine, and give God the glory, glory.
Rise and shine, and give God the glory, glory.
Rise and shine, and give God the glory, glory,
Children of the Lord.

SECOND VERSE

The Lord told Noah to build Him an arky, arky.
Lord told Noah to build Him an arky, arky.
Build it out of gopher barky, barky,
Children of the Lord.

THIRD VERSE

The animals, the animals, they came in by twosies, twosies.
The animals, the animals, they came in by twosies, twosies.
Elephants and kangaroosies, roosies,
Children of the Lord.

FOURTH VERSE

It rained and poured for forty daysies, daysies.
Rained and poured for forty daysies, daysies.
Almost drove those animals crazy, crazy,
Children of the Lord.

FIFTH VERSE

The sun came out and dried up the landy, landy.
Sun, it came out and dried up the landy, landy.
Everything was fine and dandy, dandy,
Children of the Lord.

THE B-I-B-L-E

Traditional

The B-I-B-L-E,
Yes, that's the book for me.
I stand alone on the Word of God,
The B-I-B-L-E.

MARCHING MUSIC

As you sing with the kids, march through the house in a parade and play instruments if you have them.

~DANA, 12
FARGO, ND

CHRIST THE LORD IS RISEN TODAY

by Charles Wesley

FIRST VERSE

Christ the Lord is ris'n today. Alleluia!
Sons of men and angels say: Alleluia!
Raise your joys and triumphs high. Alleluia!
Sing, ye heav'ns, and earth, reply: Alleluia!

SECOND VERSE

Lives again our glorious King. Alleluia!
Where, O death, is now thy sting? Alleluia!
Dying once, He all doth save. Alleluia!
Where thy victory, O grave? Alleluia!

THIRD VERSE

Love's redeeming work is done. Alleluia!
Fought the fight, the battle won. Alleluia!
Death in vain forbids Him rise. Alleluia!
Christ has opened paradise. Alleluia!

FOURTH VERSE

Soar we now where Christ has led. Alleluia!
Foll'wing our exalted Head. Alleluia!
Made like Him, like Him we rise. Alleluia!
Ours the cross, the grave, the skies. Alleluia!

DAVID PLAYED

by Rebecca P. Totilo

Sing to the tune of "London Bridge."

FIRST VERSE

David played the harp and sang,
harp and sang,
harp and sang.
David played the harp and sang,
All day long.

SECOND VERSE

David went to a rippling brook,
rippling brook,
rippling brook.
David went to a rippling brook,
And five stones he took.

THIRD VERSE

David's sling went round and round,
round and round,
round and round.
David's sling went round and round
And Goliath came down.

DOWN IN MY HEART

by George W. Cooke

FIRST VERSE

I've got the joy, joy, joy, joy down in my heart.
Down in my heart, down in my heart.
I've got the joy, joy, joy, joy down in my heart.
Down in my heart to stay.

SECOND VERSE

I have the peace that passeth understanding down in my heart,
Down in my heart, down in my heart.
I have the peace that passeth understanding down in my heart.
Down in my heart to stay.

THIRD VERSE

I have the love of Jesus, love of Jesus down in my heart.
Down in my heart, down in my heart.
I have the love of Jesus, love of Jesus down in my heart.
Down in my heart to stay.

FATHER ABRAHAM

Traditional

CHORUS

Father Abraham had many sons;
And many sons had Father Abraham.
I am one of them, and so are you.
So let's just praise the Lord.
Right arm!
(*move right arm as you sing next verse*)

FIRST VERSE

Right arm, left arm!
(*move both arms as you sing next verse*)

SECOND VERSE

Right arm, left arm, right foot!
(*move both arms and right foot as you sing next verse*)

THiRD VERSE

Right arm, left arm, right foot, left foot!

(*move both arms and both feet as you sing next verse*)

FOURTH VERSE

Right arm, left arm, right foot, left foot, chin up!

(*move both arms and feet and nod head as you sing next verse*)

FiFTH VERSE

Right arm, left arm, right foot, left foot, chin up, turn around!

(*move arms, feet, nod and spin around as you sing next verse*)

SiXTH VERSE

Right arm, left arm, right foot, left foot, chin up, turn around, sit down!

(*move arms, feet, nod, spin and sit down as you sing*)

FATHER, SON AND HOLY GHOST

by Rebecca P. Totilo

Sing to the tune of "Head, Shoulders, Knees and Toes."

Father, Son and Holy Ghost, Holy Ghost,
Father, Son and Holy Ghost, Holy Ghost,
They're all part of the blessed Trinity.
Father, Son and Holy Ghost, Holy Ghost.

GOD SENT HIS SON, JESUS

by Rebecca P. Totilo

Sing to the tune of "Ring Around the Rosy."

God sent His son, Jesus
To save us from our sins.
Jesus, Jesus, we all love You!

HALLELUJAH

Traditional

Hallelu, hallelu, hallelu, hallelujah!
Praise ye the Lord!
Hallelu, hallelu, hallelu, hallelujah!
Praise ye the Lord!
Praise ye the Lord, hallelujah!
Praise ye the Lord, hallelujah!
Praise ye the Lord, hallelujah!
Praise ye the Lord!

HO-HO-HO HOSANNA

Traditional

Ho, Ho, Ho, Hosanna.
Ha, Ha, Ha, Hallelujah.
He, He, He, He saved me.
I've got the joy of the Lord.

♪ I Am A "C"

Author Unknown

I am a C.
I am a C-H.
I am a C-H-R-I-S-T-I-A-N.
And I have C-H-R-I-S-T in my
H-E-A-R-T and I will
L-I-V-E E-T-E-R-N-A-L-L-Y.

∞ · ∞ · ∞ · ∞ · ∞

IF YOU'RE HAPPY AND YOU KNOW IT

Traditional

FIRST VERSE

If you're happy and you know it,
clap your hands.
If you're happy and you know it,
clap your hands.
If you're happy and you know it,
Then your face will surely show it.
If you're happy and you know it,
clap your hands.

SECOND VERSE

If you're happy and you know it,
stomp your feet.
If you're happy and you know it,
stomp your feet.
If you're happy and you know it,
Then your face will surely show it.
If you're happy and you know it,
stomp your feet.

If you're happy and you know it,
say, "Amen."
If you're happy and you know it,
say, "Amen."
If you're happy and you know it,
Then your face will surely show it.
If you're happy and you know it,
say, "Amen."

THiRD VERSE

If you're happy and you know it,
do all three.
If you're happy and you know it,
do all three.
If you're happy and you know it,
Then your face will surely show it.
If you're happy and you know it,
do all three.

i'm in THE LoRD'S ARmY

Traditional

I may never march in the infantry,
> (*march in place*)

shoot the artillery,
> (*"shoot" the enemy*)

ride in the cavalry.
> (*ride in place*)

I may never fly over the enemy,
> (*extend arms and "fly"*)

but I'm in the Lord's army. Yes, sir!
> (*salute and shout, "yes, sir!"*)

JESUS CHRIST IS THE SON OF GOD

by Rebecca P. Totilo

Sing to the tune of "London Bridge Is Falling Down."

God loved the world, so He sent His Son,
To die for us, on the cross.
Now, you and I can believe in Him.
His name is Jesus.

JESUS LOVES ME

by Anna B. Warner

FIRST VERSE

Jesus loves me this I know,
For the Bible tells me so.
Little ones to Him belong;
They are weak, but He is strong.

CHORUS

Yes, Jesus loves me.
Yes, Jesus loves me.
Yes, Jesus loves me.
The Bible tells me so.

SECOND VERSE

Jesus loves me! He who died
Heaven's gates to open wide.
He will wash away my sin,
Let His little child come in.

JONAH'S SONG

by Rebecca P. Totilo

Sing to the tune of "Arky, Arky"

FIRST VERSE

The Lord told Jonah, "Go tell Nina, Nineveh."
The Lord told Jonah, "Go tell Nina, Nineveh."
Go tell Nineveh, repent from their sins,
Children of the Lord.

SECOND VERSE

Jonah told God, "There's no way I'm going there."
Jonah told God, "There's no way I'm going there."
So Jonah took a ship and fled to the sea,
Children of the Lord.

THIRD VERSE

God sent a whale, to swallow up Jonah, Jonah.
God sent a whale, to swallow up Jonah, Jonah.
Big fat whale gulped up a Jonah, Jonah,
Children of the Lord.

FOURTH VERSE

For three whole nights, Jonah slept in there.
For three whole nights, Jonah slept in there.
Three whole nights, Jonah smelled like weedy, seaweed,
Children of the Lord.

FIFTH VERSE

Jonah told God, "Okay Lord, I'll obey You now."
Jonah told God, "Okay Lord, I'll obey You now."
Then the whale spit Jonah up on the beachy beachy,
Children of the Lord.

MY GOD IS SO GREAT

Traditional

FIRST VERSE

My God is so big,
so strong and so mighty;
There's nothing my God cannot do.
My God is so big,
so strong and so mighty;
There's nothing my God cannot do.

SECOND VERSE

He made the stars,
He made the seas,
He made the elephants, too!
My God is so big,
so strong and so mighty;
There's nothing my God cannot do.

ONLY A BOY NAMED DAVID

Traditional

FIRST VERSE

Only a boy named David,
Only a little sling,
Only a boy named David,
But he could play and sing.
Only a boy named David,
Only a rippling brook,
Only a boy named David,
But five little stones he took.

SECOND VERSE

And one little stone went in the sling,
And the sling went round and round,
And one little stone went in the sling,
And the sling went round and round,
And round and round and round and
round and round and round and round.
And one little stone went up in the air,
And the giant came tumbling down.

PETER, JAMES AND JOHN IN A SAILBOAT

Traditional

FIRST VERSE

Peter, James and John in a sailboat,
Peter, James and John in a sailboat,
Peter, James and John in a sailboat,
Down by the deep, deep sea.

SECOND VERSE

Fished all night and caught no fishes,
Fished all night and caught no fishes,
Fished all night and caught no fishes,
Down by the deep, deep sea.

THIRD VERSE

Christ came walking down by the water,
Christ came walking down by the water,
Christ came walking down by the water,
Down by the deep, deep sea.

FOURTH VERSE
Now their nets are full and breaking,
Now their nets are full and breaking,
Now their nets are full and breaking,
Down by the deep, deep sea.

FIFTH VERSE
Called their friends to come and help them,
Called their friends to come and help them,
Called their friends to come and help them,
Down by the deep, deep sea.

PRAISE Him
Traditional

FIRST VERSE
Praise Him, praise Him,
Praise Him in the morning,
Praise Him at the noontime,
Praise Him, praise Him,
Praise Him when the sun goes down.

SECOND VERSE
Love Him, love Him,
Love Him in the morning,
Love Him at the noontime,
Love Him, love Him,
Love Him when the sun goes down.

THIRD VERSE
Serve Him, serve Him,
Serve Him in the morning,

Serve Him at the noontime,
Serve Him, serve Him,
Serve Him when the sun goes down.

FOURTH VERSE

Thank Him, thank Him,
Thank Him in the morning,
Thank Him at the noontime,
Thank Him, thank Him,
Thank Him when the sun goes down.

THIS IS MY COMMANDMENT

Traditional

This is My commandment,
that you love one another,
that your joy may be full.
This is My commandment,
that you love one another,
that your joy may be full.
That your joy may be full,
that your joy may be full.
This is My commandment,
that you love one another,
that your joy may be full.

THIS LITTLE LIGHT OF MINE

Traditional

FIRST VERSE

This little light of mine,
I'm gonna let it shine.
This little light of mine,
I'm gonna let it shine.
Let it shine, let it shine, let it shine.

SECOND VERSE

Hide it under a bushel? No!
I'm gonna let it shine.
Hide it under a bushel? No!
I'm gonna let it shine.
Let it shine, let it shine, let it
shine.

THIRD VERSE

Don't let Satan blow it out,
I'm gonna let it shine.
Don't let Satan blow it out,
I'm gonna let it shine.
Let it shine, let it shine, let it shine.

FOURTH VERSE

Let it shine till Jesus comes,
I'm gonna let it shine.
Let it shine till Jesus comes,
I'm gonna let it shine.
Let it shine, let it shine, let it shine.

WHAT A MIGHTY GOD WE SERVE

Traditional

What a mighty God we serve.
What a mighty God we serve.
Angels bow before Him;
Heaven and earth adore Him.
What a mighty God we serve.

PRAYER OF PRAISE

Father, in Jesus' name, I praise and exalt You.
For You alone are worthy of our praise. I will
sing praise to Your name. Let everything that
has breath praise the Lord. Amen.
— based on Psalm 22 and Psalm 41

THE RHYTHM SECTION

CHILDREN LOVE TO MAKE NOISE! Toddlers will shake and bang any object you hand them to see what kind of noise it makes. That's the way God made us. The book of Psalms says to make a joyful noise to the Lord. Check out Psalm 150:3-5 for ways to praise Him:

> **"Praise him with the sounding of the trumpet, praise him with the harp and lyre, praise him with tambourine and dancing, praise him with the strings and flute, praise him with the clash of cymbals, praise him with resounding cymbals."**

But the constant banging of a plastic toy on the table could send you over the edge! So why not provide the children with a variety of musical instruments you can make using ordinary household items? Drums to bang and cymbals to crash are sure to be a big hit! Not to mention, you will add more fun to your sing-along while bringing praise to God.

RHYTHM SOAPBOX

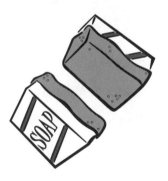

WHAT YOU NEED

◎ two bar soap boxes (full or empty)

◎ two sheets of sandpaper

◎ glue

WHAT TO DO

1. Glue a piece of sandpaper to one side of each soapbox.

2. Rub the boxes together to make fun sounds.

COFFEE CAN DRUM

WHAT YOU NEED
◎ empty coffee can with lid

◎ dry beans

WHAT TO DO

1. Fill an empty coffee can with beans.

2. Replace the lid. Tape the lid down so the beans don't fall out!

3. Shake!

∽ • ∽ ♥ ∽ ♥ ∽ • ∾

SODA CAN SHAKERS

WHAT YOU NEED

◎ empty, clean soda can

◎ dried rice or beans

◎ packing tape

◎ construction paper

◎ scissors

WHAT TO DO

1. Remove tab from empty soda can. Cut construction paper the same width as the can and wrap it around the can. Color designs on the paper.

2. Fill the can with one cup of dry rice or beans.

3. Tape over the opening with packing tape and shake!

TISSUE-BOX GUITAR

WHAT YOU NEED

◎ rectangular, empty tissue box

◎ rubber bands (various sizes and thicknesses)

WHAT TO DO

1. Stretch rubber bands across the box opening and around the long side of the box.

2. Thick rubber bands make low tones, while thin ones make higher tones. Use four or five different rubber bands on the box to get a variety of tones.

KAZOO

WHAT YOU NEED

◎ comb

◎ tissue paper

WHAT TO DO

1. Wrap tissue paper around the comb.

2. Blow!

RHYTHM GRATER AND LID CYMBALS

WHAT YOU NEED

◎ kitchen grater

◎ wooden spoon

◎ metal pot lids

WHAT TO DO

1. Strum the wooden spoon back and forth across the grater.

2. Crash the lids together like symbols.

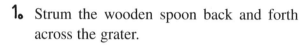

LUNCH BAG MARACAS

WHAT YOU NEED

◎ paper lunch bags

◎ yarn or rubber band

◎ markers or crayons

◎ dry beans or rice

WHAT TO DO

1. Decorate a paper bag with markers, crayons and stickers.

2. Fill the bag with dry beans and tie it closed with yarn.

3. Shake it up!

LET'S EAT!

PREPARING MEALS FOR CHILDREN may seem like a lot of work, but it can be one of the most enjoyable parts of babysitting. Enlist older children to help you set the table, make the food and clean up. Getting the kids involved adds to the fun and makes your job easier.

Some parents will leave instructions for what they would like for you to serve the children, such as peanut butter and jelly sandwiches or hot dogs. Other parents may treat you to a delivery pizza. Either way, you get the pleasure of a free meal while you earn money!

If the parents don't leave specific instructions for what they would like you to fix, try preparing something simple that you know kids love, such as spaghetti or grilled cheese sandwiches. Look at recipes for munchies on page 197 for more specific meal and snack ideas.

RULES OF THE KITCHEN

1. Gather all of the ingredients you need before you start cooking.

2. Measure out all dry and liquid ingredients to be sure you have enough of everything before you start.

3. Be very careful with sharp knives. Hold the blade pointing downward. Always use a cutting board.

4. Let young kids do safe and easy preparation tasks, like washing vegetables or sifting flour.

5. Clean as you go. Rinse dishes and place them in the dishwasher and wipe any spills right away.

6. Place hot dishes and pans on a trivet, never directly on a counter or kitchen table.

7. Don't forget to turn off the oven or stovetop when you are finished.

8. Never let children run or play with food in their mouths.

9. Cut food into small pieces for little kids. Serve drinks in plastic sip-cups to prevent spills.

10. Turn saucepan handles to the inside of the stove top, so you or the kids do not burn your hands or spill the pans.

11. Never hold a baby while working near a stove or carrying a hot drink.

BOTTLE-FEEDING A BABY

Make sure you know what, when and how to feed a baby. Even though we say that babies drink "milk," this milk is not the kind you buy in the dairy section of the grocery store. Babies less than a year old are unable to digest cow's milk. They can only drink formula or breast milk. So don't be afraid to ask the parents what type of milk they want their baby to have. Parents will appreciate your attention to detail. Here is how to bottle-feed a baby:

1. Gather all of the supplies you will need: bottle, bib and cloth diaper or small towel to drape over your shoulder when you burp the baby.

2. Prepare and warm the bottle as instructed by the parents. To warm the bottle, place it in a pan of water that has been heated on the low setting. It might seem like a good

shortcut to warm the bottle in the microwave, but the way a microwave heats (from the inside out) gets the liquid too hot in the center. You might successfully test some liquid from a microwave-warmed bottle, but the really hot liquid will be in the center of the bottle. Also, many disposable bottles could burst in a microwave.

3. After you believe the bottle liquid is warm (about 4 or 5 minutes), test it by shaking a few drops on your wrist. If it feels "lukewarm" (neither too hot nor too cold) it is ready.

4. Find a comfortable place to sit where you can rest the baby on your lap (a chair with an arm rest works well). Cradle the baby's head in the bend of your elbow, slightly higher than the baby's shoulders.

5. Tie a bib around the baby's neck to protect her clothing from spit-up or drool.

6. Place the bottle in the baby's mouth, tipping the bottle up so the formula fills the nipple. Tipping the bottle also keeps the baby from sucking air, which could cause her to have a stomach ache.

7. After the baby has finished about half of the bottle, hold the baby upright, laying the baby's head on your shoulder.

8. Tap the baby's back until you hear a burp. The baby may burp up a little formula. That's okay! If you have trouble getting a burp, lay the baby on her tummy across your lap and gently tap her back.

9. After the baby burps, give her the rest of the bottle, then try to get her to burp again. It is important that the baby burps, otherwise she could get gas pain and cry from the discomfort.

SPOON-FEEDING A BABY

Feeding a child is not all that different from feeding yourself, except it's a lot messier! Here are the steps to a fun feeding:

1. Get everything ready that you will need: bib, wash cloth, dish or feeder, baby spoon and food.

2. Place the baby in a highchair or infant seat. Make sure the safety belt is secure so they baby will not slide out.

3. Fasten the bib around the baby's neck.

4. Place a small dab of food on the spoon and slowly put it in the baby's mouth. If you are lucky, he will be hungry and have his mouth open wide like a little bird. For babies who are new to solid food, you may have to try several times to put the same spoonful of food back into his mouth. Eventually, it will go down. When a baby spits out food or makes strange faces it does not necessarily mean he doesn't like the food. It may just be a new taste he's experiencing!

5. If the baby is flailing around, making it difficult to feed him, try holding his hands down with one hand and feed him with the other. This will help avoid the baby slinging food across the room!

6. When the baby refuses to open his lips or pushes the spoon away, he is probably finished eating.

7. Wipe his hands and face with a warm, wet washcloth before removing him from the highchair.

8. Place the baby in a safe place, then clean up any spills. Be sure to have the baby sit up for 15-20 minutes after the meal so his food can digest properly.

∽ · ∽ ♥ ∽ ♥ ∽ · ∽

MEALTIME FOR TODDLERS

Expect nothing less than a mess when toddlers eat! Finger painting with ketchup and sticking green beans in their nostrils are all part of the meal experience for curious, playful toddlers. Here are some tips for feeding toddlers:

1. Have the meal ready before placing the toddler in the highchair.

2. Make sure the toddler is strapped into the highchair and the tray is securely attached.

3. Use plastic cups and plates in case the toddler decides to toss them on the floor.

4. Cut food into small pieces.

5. If a toddler wants to feed himself, let him.

6. Use a mat or towel under the highchair to catch spills and make clean-up easier.

7. Wipe the toddler's hands and face with a warm washcloth before removing him from the highchair.

I can do everything through him who gives me strength.
~ *Philippians 4:13*

195

WHAT A MESS!

Instead of letting the children scamper off while you clean the kitchen, recruit everyone to help out after the meal. Even toddlers as young as two years old can help place spoons and forks in the dishwasher while older kids rinse off plates and cups. Children love to feel needed and are eager to show you how their family "does it."

Try to make a game out of cleaning by adding a timer. Call it the "cleanup clock." Tell everyone his or her job and try to finish cleaning before the clock buzzes. Allow kids who don't want to cooperate with the clean-up game to have a choice of chores. Ask, "Do you want to put away the silverware or wipe the table?" That way they still feel like they have some control over the situation.

If none of the kids want to help clean, try dangling a carrot in front of them. Say something like, "If we finish cleaning up the kitchen by 6:30, we'll have time to watch a video."

NOW, I'm HUNGRY

Oops! You forgot to grab something to eat before running out the door. Now the kids are asleep and you are starving! You've got your eyes set on the Italian sub sandwich in the refrigerator. It's best not to touch it, though. It might be for someone's lunch tomorrow! Instead, make a light snack from peanut butter and crackers or cereal and milk. Parents don't mind your snacking. This is one of the fringe benefits of babysitting! Try to remember to ask the parents what's okay to munch, but if you forget, eat lightly and save your appetite for when you get home.

RECiPES FOR MunCHiES

Kids can be fussy eaters! One way to get them to eat healthy food is to disguise it and serve it in fun ways. At the same time, the kids will be learning and experiencing the Bible in a whole new way. Use your *Babysitter Bible Themes* for ideas on what to serve. For instance, if your theme is Moses and the Ten Commandments, try making Moses' Burning Bush for snack time. The kids will love these edible lessons about the Bible and God's love.

AnTS on A LoG

Hard-working ants are a great example of how we should be!

WHAT YOU nEED

◎ celery

◎ peanut butter

◎ raisins

WHAT TO DO

1. Wash the celery and cut it into 3" lengths.

2. Spread peanut butter in the center of a celery section.

3. Top with raisins, spaced evenly so they look like ants crawling across the celery.

BE A CUT-UP!

Small kids can choke on round foods. Cut food like hot dogs or grapes into half-circles so they can swallow it better.

~TiFFAnY, 12
SALT LAKE CiTY, UT

BABY JESUS SALAD

Jesus understands us because He was a baby and a child, too.

WHAT YOU NEED

◎ iceberg lettuce leaf

◎ canned pear halves

◎ raisins

◎ carrot, cut into short sticks

◎ grape

WHAT TO DO

1. Place a lettuce leaf on a plate.

2. Place the pear half as the body, the grape as the head, carrot sticks as arms and legs, and raisins as the belly button, hands and feet.

3. Enjoy while sharing about the birth of Jesus.

ELIJAH'S CHARIOT WHEELS

God is there to lift us up!

WHAT YOU NEED

◎ sliced English muffins

◎ bottled pizza sauce

◎ mozzarella cheese

◎ pepperoni

◎ garlic powder

WHAT TO DO

1. Heat the oven broiler. Place the English muffins on a baking sheet and lightly toast for 1 or 2 minutes.

2. Remove the muffins from the oven. Preheat the oven to 350 degrees.

3. Spoon pizza sauce onto each muffin half and spread over the entire surface using the back of the spoon.

4. Sprinkle a layer of cheese on the sauce.

5. Cut the pepperoni into strips and place them on the pizzas like spokes on a chariot wheel. Sprinkle with salt, pepper and garlic powder.

6. Bake for 8-10 minutes or until cheese is bubbly.

FIRST FRUITS ICES

As a way of showing thanks, we should offer God our "first fruits."

WHAT YOU NEED

◎ fruit juice (any flavor)

◎ fresh strawberries or blueberries

◎ plastic cups

◎ craft sticks (optional)

WHAT TO DO

1. Pour the juice into the cups.

2. Drop a piece of fruit inside each cup. Freeze.

3. For holders, insert craft sticks in the cups before the juice is completely frozen.

FISHES AND LOAVES SNACK MIX

God can do amazing things! He will always provide for us.

WHAT YOU NEED

- ◎ non-stick cooking spray
- ◎ 2 cups rice cereal squares
- ◎ 1 cup goldfish-shaped crackers
- ◎ 1 cup pretzels
- ◎ 1 cup dry roasted peanuts
- ◎ 1 tablespoon creamy peanut butter
- ◎ 1 tablespoon honey
- ◎ 1 tablespoon apple juice
- ◎ 1 teaspoon vanilla
- ◎ ½ cup raisins

WHAT TO DO

1. Preheat the oven to 250 degrees. Lightly spray a cookie sheet with non-stick cooking spray.

2. Combine the cereal, goldfish crackers, pretzels and peanuts in a large bowl and set aside.

3. In a microwavable dish, combine the peanut butter, honey and apple juice. Microwave at high for 30 seconds. Stir in vanilla.

4. Drizzle the peanut butter mixture over the cereal and toss lightly to coat evenly.

5. Spread the mixture into a single layer on the baking sheet. Bake 8-10 minutes. Stir, then bake for another 10 minutes, until golden brown. Remove to cool.

6. Add raisins to the mixture.

JONAH'S WHALE OF A SANDWICH

God wants to use you, too!

WHAT YOU NEED

◎ pita bread

◎ lettuce leaves

◎ tomatoes

◎ ham slices

◎ mustard or mayonnaise

WHAT TO DO

1. Cut pita bread in half and open the pocket.

2. Spread mustard or mayonnaise inside the pocket and fill with ham, lettuce and tomatoes.

3. Add salt and pepper or another seasoning, if you like.

SUN SIPPERS

Jesus can do anything! Even raise Lazarus from the dead!

WHAT YOU NEED

◎ half of a seedless orange

◎ plastic drinking straw

◎ resealable sandwich bag

WHAT TO DO

1. Place the orange in the sandwich bag. Squeeze the air out and seal the bag.

2. Squeeze or stand on the orange to get the juice out.

3. Open a corner slightly and slip the straw in. Enjoy!

MANNA BURGERS

All good things come from God.

WHAT YOU NEED

◎ rice cakes

◎ peanut butter

◎ honey

WHAT TO DO

1. Allow the kids to spread peanut butter and honey on rice cakes.

2. Serve with potato chips and a pickle. Munch away!

MOSES' BURNING BUSH

God can speak to us, too!

WHAT YOU NEED

◎ 12-ounce package butterscotch or chocolate chips

◎ ½ cup peanut butter

◎ ½ cup marshmallow cream

◎ 6-ounce can fried chow mein noodles

◎ red food coloring

◎ non-stick cooking spray

1. Pour the butterscotch or chocolate chips and the peanut butter into a saucepan. Cook on low heat until it is melted. Add several drops of red food coloring.

2. Remove the saucepan from the heat. Add chow mein noodles and peanuts. Stir well.

3. Spray a cookie sheet with cooking spray. Drop spoonfuls of the mixture onto the cookie sheet. Let stand until firm.

NOAH'S FRUIT BOAT

God promises to protect us, just like
He did for Noah.

WHAT YOU NEED

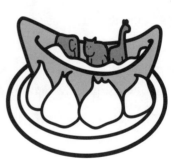

◎ melon

◎ 2 cups whipped topping

◎ blue and green food coloring

◎ animal crackers

WHAT TO DO

1. Slice the melon into wedges and remove the skin.

2. In one bowl, mix 1 cup of whipped topping and several drops of blue food coloring. In another bowl, mix 1 cup of whipped topping and several drops of green food coloring.

3. Place a melon wedge on a plate and spoon the blue whipped topping around it to create water. Use the green whipped topping inside the melon as "glue" to hold the animal crackers inside the "ark."

PETER'S CATCH OF THE DAY

Jesus said, "Follow Me, and I will make you fishers of men."

WHAT YOU NEED

- ◎ sliced white or wheat bread
- ◎ fish-shaped cookie cutter
- ◎ ½ cup peanut butter
- ◎ 2 tablespoons vegetable oil

WHAT TO DO

1. Preheat the oven to 350 degrees.

2. Use a fish-shaped cookie cutter to cut fish shapes from the bread. Set the scraps aside.

3. Place the fish flat on a baking sheet. Toast lightly in the oven for 5 or 6 minutes.

4. Place the scraps on another baking sheet and bake for 8 to 10 minutes until golden brown.

5. Grind the bread scraps into crumbs with a blender or by hand. Pour the crumbs into a shallow bowl.

6. Heat the peanut butter and oil in a saucepan until blended. Dip the toasted fish in the mixture until they are completely covered, then coat them with some of the bread crumbs.

7. Lay the fish flat on a baking sheet until dry.

TERRIFIC TIP!

ANIMAL FOOD

When you can't get the kids to eat, try setting places at the table for the kids' favorite stuffed animals. When the kids see their animals "eat," they will, too!

~CHLOE, 13
SAN LUIS OBISPO, CA

QUEEN OF HEARTS COOKIES

Like Queen Esther, you'll win friends hands down when you deal the kids one of these crisp cookies.

WHAT YOU NEED

- ◎ 2 cups sifted flour
- ◎ 1¼ teaspoon baking powder
- ◎ ¼ teaspoon salt
- ◎ ⅓ cup soft butter
- ◎ ¾ cup sugar
- ◎ 1 egg
- ◎ ½ teaspoon vanilla extract
- ◎ 2 teaspoons milk
- ◎ red food coloring
- ◎ non-stick cooking spray
- ◎ cookie sheet
- ◎ rolling pin
- ◎ spatula
- ◎ cutting board

WHAT TO DO

1. Preheat the oven to 400 degrees. Mix the flour, baking powder and salt in a large bowl.

2. In another bowl, cream the butter and sugar together. Beat in the egg, milk and vanilla extract. Blend well.

3. Slowly add the dry ingredients to the butter mixture, until well blended.

4. Place the dough in the refrigerator until it is firm enough to handle.

5. Set aside a third of the dough in another bowl. Keep it in the refrigerator until you are ready to use it for the hearts.

6. Sprinkle a little flour on a clean cutting board and put the dough on the board. Lightly dust the rolling pin with flour and flatten the dough. Use a playing card as your guide to cut out rectangles shapes.

7. Lift the cookie using a spatula, and place it on the sprayed cookie sheet.

8. Remove the extra dough from the refrigerator. Add several drops of red food coloring and mix well. Again, flatten the dough using the rolling pin. Cut out small hearts that will fit on the rectangles.

9. Lift the hearts and place one in the center of each rectangle cookie. Press down lightly.

10. Bake for 8 - 10 minutes, until golden brown. Allow to cool on a plate before serving.

•••••••••••••••••••••••••••••••••••••

Taste and see that the Lord is good.
~ Psalm 34:8

ROCK CANDY

You can make this with the children and leave it with them so they can watch the crystals grow. Or you might want to make it in advance and use it as a fun snack.

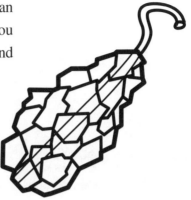

WHAT YOU NEED

◎ 2 cups sugar

◎ 1 cup water

◎ stainless steel washer

◎ large, clean glass jar

◎ white string

◎ pencil

◎ spoon

◎ teakettle

WHAT TO DO

1. Fill the jar with sugar.

2. Fill the teakettle with water and bring it to a boil. Carefully, pour the hot water into the jar, wetting the sugar. Press down the sugar with a spoon, making sure it gets completely wet. Continue to add water until the jar is filled and the sugar is completely dissolved.

3. Cut the string about the same length as the jar. Tie one end around the pencil and the other end around the washer.

4. Straddle the pencil across the mouth of the jar with the string dangling down into the sugar-water mixture.

5. Set the jar, uncovered, in a place where it will be undisturbed for a few days. Rock candy crystals will begin to form on the string and jar within a few hours. If a crystal sheet forms across the opening of the jar, break it up so the rock crystals can continue to grow.

SAMUEL'S BEDROLL

We should always listen to God and do what He says.

WHAT YOU NEED

◎ 2 tablespoons mayonnaise

◎ 2 tablespoons mustard

◎ 2 teaspoons chopped green onion tops

◎ 4 large pretzel logs or bread sticks

◎ 8 thin, round slices ham or turkey breast

◎ plastic wrap

WHAT TO DO

1. Combine the mayonnaise, mustard and green onion in a small bowl. Mix well.

2. Arrange two turkey or ham slices on a large sheet of plastic wrap, overlapping the slices in the center. Spread a fourth of the mayonnaise mixture evenly onto the slices, covering them completely.

3. Place one pretzel at the bottom edge of the turkey or ham slice and roll it up around the pretzel.

4. Repeat with the remaining ingredients.

THUMBPRINT COOKIES

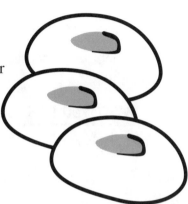

Everyone is special to God!

WHAT YOU NEED

- ½ cup peanut butter
- 1 cup shortening
- ½ cup white sugar
- ⅔ cup firmly packed brown sugar
- 1 large egg
- 1 teaspoon vanilla extract
- 1 cup flour
- ½ teaspoon salt
- 1 teaspoon baking soda
- 1 teaspoon cinnamon
- non-stick cooking spray

WHAT TO DO

1. Preheat the oven to 350 degrees. Spray the cookie sheet with non-stick cooking spray.

2. Mix the peanut butter, shortening, white sugar and ½ cup of the brown sugar in a large bowl. Blend mixture until it is creamy.

3. Add the egg and vanilla to the creamy mixture and beat until well blended.

4. In another bowl, stir the flour, salt, and baking soda. Add to the creamy mixture. Blend well.

5. Use a teaspoon to spoon dough into a hand and roll into balls.

6. In a shallow dish, mix together the cinnamon and remaining brown sugar. Roll the balls in the mixture.

7. Place the balls on the cookie sheet. Have the kids flatten the balls with a thumb to leave their prints.

8. Bake for 8 to 10 minutes, until golden brown.

TOWER OF BABEL STACKS

God can help us to be patient and understanding!

WHAT YOU NEED

◎ round crackers

◎ cheese

◎ ham

◎ turkey

WHAT TO DO

1. This is a fun snack for kids. Allow them to build a tall "sandwich tower" with the crackers, cheese and meat.

2. After the towers are finished, enjoy eating your creations!

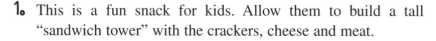

KIDS CAFÉ

Make menus for your meal with a few choices and let the kids order from it. They will like pretending that they are in a restaurant.

~JALEESA, 12
PHILADELPHIA, PA

WEIGHT-LIFTING SNACKS

When God lives on the inside of us,
we can be strong!

WHAT YOU NEED

◎ large marshmallows

◎ thin pretzel sticks

◎ chocolate syrup (optional)

WHAT TO DO

1. Slide a marshmallow onto each end of a pretzel.

2. Squeeze chocolate syrup on a plate and roll the marshmallows in it. Chill in the refrigerator for a couple minutes.

3. Enjoy while reading the story about Samson's incredible strength to the children.

WOODEN CROSS & PRAYING HANDS PRETZELS

When we pray, we should look to
the cross for our help!

WHAT YOU NEED

◎ non-stick cooking spray

◎ 1 can refrigerated bread sticks/bread dough

◎ 1 egg white

◎ 2 teaspoons water

◎ sea salt

◎ Italian seasoning

WHAT TO DO

1. Preheat the oven to 375 degrees. Spray non-stick cooking spray on a baking sheet.

2. Remove bread dough from package and roll out into thin ropes on a clean counter top.

3. Form praying hands by crossing the ends over. You can also make a cross with two ropes.

4. Place the shapes on the baking sheet.

5. Beat together the egg white and water until foamy. Lightly brush the pretzels with the egg mixture, sprinkle with course salt and seasoning. Bake for 10 minutes.

A PRAYER BEFORE EATING

Father, bless this food we are about to receive for our bodies. Thank You for it and help us to remember all those who are in need. In Jesus' name, Amen.

RECIPE FOR FUN

You can make edible play clay by mixing 2 cups of powdered dry milk, 2 cups of creamy peanut butter and a cup of honey. Blend it well, then give each kid a clump of dough. Decorate with sprinkles, colored candies or raisins. It's fun and yummy!

~ZOE, 12
BLOOMINGTON, IN

SHARE YOUR FAITH

WITNESSING, OR TELLING OTHERS ABOUT JESUS, is not as scary as you might think. Most people are curious and want to know why you are full of joy despite the tough situations you might face. It's easy! Just tell others about what God has done for you.

When you babysit, you have the opportunity to share with the children (and sometimes even the parents) about the Lord. God will lead you and be with you.

Don't know what to say? Share your personal testimony. Tell them what God has done in your life. This should feel comfortable since you're talking about yourself. As you read Bible stories and do the crafts and activities included in this book, you will be teaching the children about God.

Listed below are some helpful scriptures for witnessing. Use these as you explain why we all need God in our lives and what Jesus did on the cross for us.

SCRIPTURES FOR WITNESSING

For God so loved the world that he gave his one and only Son, that whoever believes in him shall not perish but have eternal life.

~ John 3:16

For all have sinned and fall short of the glory of God.

~ Romans 3:23

But God demonstrates his own love for us in this: While we were still sinners, Christ died for us.

~ Romans 5:8

For the wages of sin is death, but the gift of God is eternal life in Christ Jesus our Lord.

~ Romans 6:23

That if you confess with your mouth, "Jesus is Lord," and believe in your heart that God raised him from the dead, you will be saved.

~ Romans 10:9-10

By grace you have been saved, through faith – and this is not from yourselves, it is a gift from God.

~ Ephesians 2:8

If we confess our sins, he is faithful and just and will forgive us our sins and purify us from all unrighteousness.

~ 1 John 1:9

He who has the Son has life; he who does not have the Son of God does not have life. I write these things to you who believe in the name of the Son of God so that you may know that you have eternal life.

~ 1 John 5:12-13

I stand at the door and knock. If anyone hears my voice and opens the door, I will come in and eat with him, and he with me.

~ Revelation 3:20

PRAYER OF COMMITMENT

Father, I commit myself to do your will today. Fill my mind with a clear knowledge of Your will. I will not rely on my own insight but in all my ways I will acknowledge You. I will listen only to Your voice. Lead me in the way I should go. Amen.

BABYSITTING FORMS & FUN

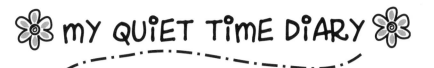

MY QUIET TIME DIARY

Date:_____

The Scripture I read today:_____

What is God saying?_____

_____

What does it mean to me?_____

_____

· ·

Date:_____

The Scripture I read today:_____

What is God saying?_____

_____

What does it mean to me?_____

_____

· ·

Date:_____

The Scripture I read today:_____

What is God saying?_____

_____

What does it mean to me?_____

_____

Date:_____

The Scripture I read today:_____

What is God saying?_____

_____

What does it mean to me?_____

_____

....

Date:_____

The Scripture I read today:_____

What is God saying?_____

_____

What does it mean to me?_____

_____

....

Date:_____

The Scripture I read today:_____

What is God saying?_____

_____

What does it mean to me?_____

_____

Date:_____

The Scripture I read today:_____

What is God saying?_____

_____

What does it mean to me?_____

_____

....

Date:_____

The Scripture I read today:_____

What is God saying?_____

_____

What does it mean to me?_____

_____

....

Date:_____

The Scripture I read today:_____

What is God saying?_____

_____

What does it mean to me?_____

_____

Date:_____

The Scripture I read today:_____

What is God saying?_____

_____

What does it mean to me?_____

_____

••

Date:_____

The Scripture I read today:_____

What is God saying?_____

_____

What does it mean to me?_____

_____

••

Date:_____

The Scripture I read today:_____

What is God saying?_____

_____

What does it mean to me?_____

_____

Date:_____

The Scripture I read today:_____

What is God saying?_____

_____

What does it mean to me?_____

_____

· ·

Date:_____

The Scripture I read today:_____

What is God saying?_____

_____

What does it mean to me?_____

_____

· ·

Date:_____

The Scripture I read today:_____

What is God saying?_____

_____

What does it mean to me?_____

_____

Date:_____

The Scripture I read today:_____

What is God saying?_____

_____

What does it mean to me?_____

_____

· ·

Date:_____

The Scripture I read today:_____

What is God saying?_____

_____

What does it mean to me?_____

_____

· ·

Date:_____

The Scripture I read today:_____

What is God saying?_____

_____

What does it mean to me?_____

_____

Date:_____

The Scripture I read today:_____

What is God saying?_____

_____

What does it mean to me?_____

_____

··

Date:_____

The Scripture I read today:_____

What is God saying?_____

_____

What does it mean to me?_____

_____

··

Date:_____

The Scripture I read today:_____

What is God saying?_____

_____

What does it mean to me?_____

_____

Date:_____

The Scripture I read today:_____

What is God saying?_____

_____

What does it mean to me?_____

_____

....

Date:_____

The Scripture I read today:_____

What is God saying?_____

_____

What does it mean to me?_____

_____

....

Date:_____

The Scripture I read today:_____

What is God saying?_____

_____

What does it mean to me?_____

_____

Date:_____

The Scripture I read today:_____

What is God saying?_____

_____

What does it mean to me?_____

_____

....

Date:_____

The Scripture I read today:_____

What is God saying?_____

_____

What does it mean to me?_____

_____

....

Date:_____

The Scripture I read today:_____

What is God saying?_____

_____

What does it mean to me?_____

_____

Date:_____

The Scripture I read today:_____

What is God saying?_____

_____

What does it mean to me?_____

_____

···

Date:_____

The Scripture I read today:_____

What is God saying?_____

_____

What does it mean to me?_____

_____

···

Date:_____

The Scripture I read today:_____

What is God saying?_____

_____

What does it mean to me?_____

_____

_____'s

Babysitting Calendar

_____

Sunday	Monday	Tuesday	Wednesday	Thursday	Friday	Saturday

THE BABYSITTER'S BIO

The parents and family will be interested in knowing about you. Here is an evaluation tool to help you prepare for any questions they may ask. Check or fill in the answers to help you discover your skills, abilities, likes and dislikes regarding babysitting. Don't give it to the parents, just use it to help you learn more about yourself. Update your bio every three months.

How many years I have been a Christian:

○ 1-3   ○ 4-6   ○ 7-10   ○ All my life

The church my family attends: _____

How many times I have volunteered to help in the church nursery or other Sunday school programs for young children:

○ 1-3   ○ 4-6   ○ 7-10   ○ Too many times to count

Number of younger brothers and sisters I have babysat for my mom and dad:

○ 0   ○ 1   ○ 2   ○ 3   ○ 4   ○ 5

The age I best like to babysit:

○ 0-2   ○ 3-5   ○ 6-10   ○ All ages

The youngest child I have ever cared for was a:

○ baby (newborn to 12 months)

○ toddler (1 to 3 years)

○ preschooler (3 to 5 years)

○ school-aged child (5 to 10 years)

The number of babysitting jobs I have had is:

O None, but I'm working on it.

O 1-3

O 4-6

O 7-10

O Too many to count

The most children I have watched at one time is:

O 1

O 2

O 3

O 4

O 5

O I stopped counting after 6.

I prefer to babysit for:

O Only one child. I like doing things one-on-one.

O Several children at once. It's like having a party.

O Babies. They're cute and sleep a lot.

O Toddlers. Chasing them around is cheap exercise!

O Preschoolers. Everything amazes them.

O School-aged children. I can relate to this age best.

The longest I have ever babysat was:

O 1 hour

O 2 to 3 hours

○ 3 to 5 hours

○ 5 to 8 hours

○ Over 8 hours

Ĭ have accepted babysitting jobs (check all that apply):

○ at night

○ during the day

○ on weekends

○ on school nights

Ĭ prefer to babysit:

○ at night

○ during the day

○ on weekends

○ on school nights

Ĭ like getting rides to and from babysitting jobs from:

○ my parents

○ the child's parents

○ on my own

my parents will (check all that apply):

○ Support my decision to start a babysitting business.

○ Pray for my safety and protection while I'm babysitting.

○ Provide rides to and from my babysitting jobs.

○ Make the final decision of which jobs I can accept.

○ Be available if I need help while at a job.

I charge $ _____ per hour for babysitting.

Emergency situations I have handled:

_____

_____

_____

_____

Additional babysitting training or first-aid courses I have taken:

_____

_____

_____

_____

BEFORE i LEAVE HOME

1. Client's name: _____

Address _____

Phone _____

2. Directions to Client's Home:

_____

_____

_____

_____

_____

_____

_____

_____

3. Who will take me to the job: _____

   Time: _____

4. Who will bring me home after the job: _____

   Time: _____

5. Prayer needs for the children: _____

_____

_____

GETTING TO KNOW YOU

BASIC AND EMERGENCY INFORMATION

Family's name: _____

Children's names and ages:

_____   _____

_____   _____

_____   _____

_____   _____

Pets' names:

_____   _____

_____   _____

Address: _____

Nearest cross street: _____

Security system keypad code and password: _____

Emergency number (if not 911): _____

In case of emergency, please contact: _____

                       relationship _____

                       phone _____

Parent's cell phone or pager: _____

Doctor: _____

Address: _____

Hospital: _____

Address: _____

Poison Control: _____

Nearest neighbor: _____

Address: _____

Phone: _____

Any special needs, allergies or medical information for a child?

_____

_____

Any medication to be given? How much and what time?

_____

_____

Ask parents about the location of the following:

○ Telephones
○ Smoke alarms
○ Emergency exits and ladders
○ Fire extinguishers
○ Flashlights
○ First-aid kit
○ Extra set of house keys
○ Circuit breaker or fuse box
○ Diaper disposal

HOUSE RULES

What types of discipline work best with this child, if necessary?

_____

_____

Are there any rooms in the house that are "off limits"?

_____

_____

What chores does the child need to do?

_____

May the child watch TV?

○ yes   ○ no

Are any channels forbidden? _____

Can the child watch videos?

○ yes   ○ no

Are the child's friends allowed to visit?

○ yes   ○ no

Who? _____

Can they come inside?

○ yes   ○ no

Can the child go to a friend's house?

○ yes   ○ no

Which friends? _____

Can the child use the phone?

○ yes   ○ no

Where may the child play?

○ front yard ○ back yard ○ bedroom   ○ living room

Will the pet(s) require any food or special care? Does it stay inside or outside?

_____

_____

BEDTiME

Does the child take a nap? What time? How long?

_____

_____

What will help the child fall asleep?

_____

_____

Does the child use a pacifier when sleeping?

○ yes   ○ no

Does the child have a special blanket or stuffed animal for sleeping?

○ blanket   ○ stuffed animal

How does the child prefer the door to be able to sleep?

○ open   ○ closed

How does the child prefer the lights when sleeping?

○ on ○ off

Does the child use a night light?

○ yes ○ no

Is the child afraid of the dark?

○ yes ○ no

When is bedtime? _____

Can the child have a bedtime snack?

○ yes ○ no

Are there any special bedtime routines?

_____

_____

Can I pray with the children before bed?

_____

mEALTimE

Does the child have food allergies?

○ yes ○ no

If so, what? _____

Does the child have a restricted diet?

○ vegetarian ○ kosher ○ no salt ○ no milk products

○ no sugar ○ diabetic (get specific instructions)

When are mealtimes?

Breakfast: _____

Lunch: _____

Dinner: _____

Are there any special dishes, spoons or bibs I should use for meals?

_____

_____

Can the child feed himself or herself?

○ yes   ○ no

What would you like for me to serve the children?

_____

Any special equipment in the kitchen I will need to use and how do I operate it?

_____

_____

Is it okay if I cook or bake?

○ yes   ○ no

What does the baby drink from the bottle?

○ milk   ○ formula

The bottle should be served...

○ heated. If so, how? _____

○ room temperature.

○ ice cold, straight from the refrigerator.

Does the baby eat solid foods?

○ yes   ○ no

If so, how much? _____

With a feeder or a spoon? _____

BATHTIME

Do I need to give the child a bath?

○ yes   ○ no

What time? _____

Can the children bathe together?

○ yes   ○ no

Where are the towels, soap and shampoo?

_____

_____

Do I stay in the bathroom with the older children?

○ yes   ○ no

Is the child potty-trained?

○ yes   ○ no

In training?

○ yes   ○ no

Does the child wear a diaper to bed?

○ yes   ○ no

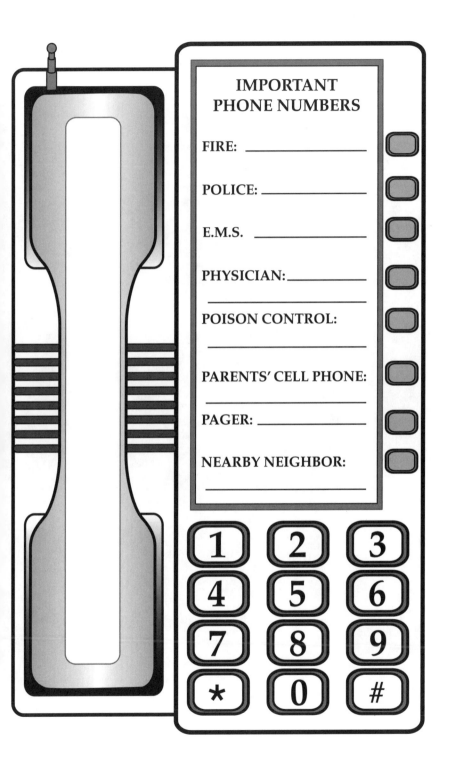

IMPORTANT
PHONE NUMBERS

FIRE: _____

POLICE: _____

E.M.S. _____

PHYSICIAN:_____
_____

POISON CONTROL:
_____

PARENTS' CELL PHONE:
_____

PAGER: _____

NEARBY NEIGHBOR:
_____

1 2 3
4 5 6
7 8 9
* 0 #

mEDiCAL TREATmEnT ConSEnT FORm

Have a parent fill in this form in case a child needs immediate medical treatment at the hospital.

I authorize any necessary and appropriate medical care for my minor child:

child's name: _____

birth date:_____

blood type: _____

allergies: _____

including X-ray, anesthetic, medical and surgical diagnosis and treatment, and hospitalization under the supervision of a licensed physician or surgeon in the state of _____. I assume full financial responsibility for medical and surgical care provided. Please contact me as soon as possible after my child is brought in for treatment.

Parent's signature: _____

Date: _____

EMERGENCY PLAN

Draw X's on the house where emergency exits are located. Draw dashed lines to the nearest exits upstairs and downstairs.

BABYSITTER'S REPORT

Date: _____

What time will the parents be home? _____

Where will the parents be? _____

Address: _____

Phone number: _____

PHONE MESSAGES

Date/Time: _____

Name: _____

Message: _____

_____

Date/Time: _____

Name: _____

Message: _____

_____

Date/Time: _____

Name: _____

Message: _____

_____

CHILD'S BEHAVIOR

○ Good   ○ Poor

Any incidents? _____

_____

Any illnesses or accidents?_____

_____

What time was the baby's diaper
changed or what time did the child last
go to the toilet? _____

Anything unusual? _____

What time did the child eat? What did the child eat? How much?

_____

_____

_____

What time did the child take a nap and/or go to bed? How long
was the nap? _____

Any other comments? _____

_____

_____

JOURNALS JUST FOR YOU!

Get serious about the Bible and have fun at the same time! These journals will help you want to dig into the Word. And the stories and writing space will help you to think, praise, pray and grow. Choose from *My Bible Journal*, complete from Genesis-Revelation; *My Prayer Journal*, tips and hints for a better prayer life; *My Answer Journal,* real kids' questions about God; *My Wisdom Journal*, advice from Proverbs; or (not pictured) *My Praise Journal*, a celebration of Psalms.

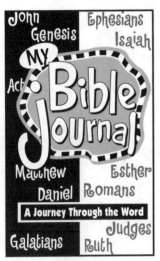

LP46911
ISBN 1-885358-70-9

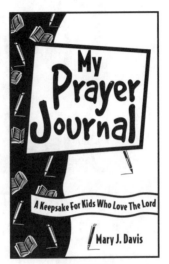

DB46731
ISBN 1-885358-37-7

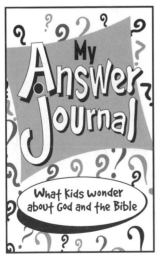

LP46931
ISBN 1-885358-72-5

LP46941
ISBN 1-885358-73-3

GET COOKING IN THE WORD WITH GOBBLE UP THE BIBLE!

For ages 5-12, this cookbook will help you learn to make really great food and grow closer to God as you do it. Each of the more than 70 recipes includes a fun activity. Includes a bonus section on kitchen safety and basic cooking techniques. FREE set of measuring spoons attached to each book!

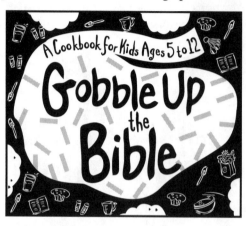

LP46811
ISBN 1-885358-59-8

YOU'RE NOT JUST A GIRL. YOU'RE ONE OF GOD'S GIRLS!

Hey, girls, get ready to add some sparkle to your look and a lot of fun to your life. *God's Girls* is packed with tips and ideas to help you make cool crafts. Plus you will read about Bible women and learn how to be a faithful Christian. There is even space included for you to write your deepest thoughts and dreams. So come on and join the party…you are one of *God's Girls!*

LP48011
ISBN 1-58411-020-1

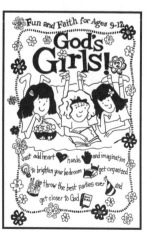

LP48012
ISBN 1-58411-021-X

THE FUN DEVOTIONAL THAT HELPS GIRLS GROW CLOSER TO GOD.

God and Me! is a series of devotionals for girls. Each age-level book is packed with over 100 devotionals, plus memory verses, stories, journal space and fun activities to help you learn more about the Bible.

LP46823
ISBN 1-885358-54-7

LP46822
ISBN 1-885358-60-1

National Best-sellers!

LP46821
ISBN 1-885358-61-X

VISIT YOUR FAVORITE CHRISTIAN BOOKSTORE TO FIND OTHER LEGACY PRESS BOOKS CREATED JUST FOR YOU.